W9-BEJ-926

# CELEBRATING THE

# AMERICAN REVOLUTION

# -

# MUNICIPAL SYMBOLS OF A

# FREE COUNTRY

Compiled By Marvin Bubie

CELEBRATING THE AMERICAN REVOLUTION – MUNICIPAL SYMBOLS OF A FREE COUNTRY

Copyright © 2011 by Marvin Bubie

All rights reserved. No part of this book may be used or reproduced in any manner whatsoever without written permission from the author except in the case of brief quotations embodied in critical articles and reviews.

To order more copies of this book, go to www.mnobooks.com

Published by MNOBOOKS, Averill Park NY 12018

Printed in the United States of America

ISBN: 978-0-615-50708-8

# DEDICATION

I love this country and the freedoms we enjoy.  I also have the highest respect for those who wear the uniform and stand on the line in defense of those freedoms as well as their families who sacrifice the presence of their loved ones for extended periods of time.

Active military families share a unique awareness of those not present on a continuous basis and very few are taken for granted.  Our freedoms should not be taken for granted either.

Municipal seals are symbols of power and authority.  The study of early wax seals is known as sigillography.  The freedom to choose those symbols is one that so universally accepted in this country it is almost invisible. Every one is a statement of freedom.

This book is a love letter to my country and in some way, is dedicated to all those who serve or who have ever served and their families, but it is especially dedicated to my family, my wife, Nancy.


Special Acknowledgements:  Proofreaders are indispensable and my heartfelt thanks to Mary Johnson for her suggestions.  I am especially grateful for the whole-hearted encouragement and support for my projects of my cousin Arleen and her husband Bill Moran, friends Jim and Charlene Cooper, friends Warren and Mary Johnson, my sister Janet and her husband Bob Laporta, our nephew Andrew Bocca and especially my wife Nancy.

# DISCLAIMERS

The histories here are those written by the municipalities themselves. Some are based on local legend rather than historical facts and I have endeavored to identify them as such. In all cases, I have tried to use seals which illustrate the history of the community and its role in the Revolutionary War. Some of the seals that I used have been replaced by newer seals that more accurately reflect the municipality and its current history. Some seals are not Revolutionary War in nature but had to be included. Boston, Philadelphia, Charleston and Savannah all have histories that must be included even if their symbols are not specifically reflective of the revolution.

DATES – There are many dates on the seals and logos themselves and this can be confusing. They can signify the date the municipality was settled, or when the charter was granted or some other event. The date I chose for the book is the date of the Revolutionary War event associated with the municipality.

GRAMMER – In compiling this book, I have intentionally used sources which use original quotations and municipal records that use colonial spellings, punctuation and capitalizations.

Although most illustrations are seals there are a few that are logos or in the case of June 14, 1777, it is our Flag. It appears on several seals after it was adopted.

Logos were used when they were more appropriate to the book, so Richmond and Plympton are examples of logos and not official seals.

Charlestown, MA, is now a part of the City of Boston, but it had a story and it had a seal at one time so it was also used even though it is now extinct.

Although I have also tried to include every municipality with a Revolutionary War history and a seal, it is inevitable that I have missed some and I extend my apologies where my research has fallen short.

Official seals and logos are almost always covered by local copyrights and laws cover inappropriate uses.

Finally, the use of any seal in this book does not imply that this book is in any way endorsed by any municipality.

# FOREWORD

Our country's birth was long and difficult and not assured until George Washington decided not to run for a third term. Danger was everywhere for 8 long years. The stakes were high and everyone knew it. Over 11,500 prisoners died aboard prison ships when they could have been freed provided they renounced their country and fought against their neighbors. The war was won on principles so high we can still to this day argue over what it means to be free.

This book is a celebration of the American Revolution, and a celebration of a unique freedom that resulted from it and of how Americans view civic identity.

Each town, city, borough, county and village listed here has a proud heritage of their participation in one of the most significant events in the history of our country and in the history of the world. Evidence of the sacrifice of our early citizen soldiers are all around us. They display that heritage on their seals.

After July 4, 1776, colonial seals designed by monarchies were discarded. From 1776 on in America, that role was omitted from our federal government and by default left to the closest form of government to the people. So, we the people get a say in our official identity and as usual in our pluralistic society, the range of our official seals is as limitless as our imaginations.

Just as we overthrew the monarchy and established a new kind of government and a new kind of social hierarchy based on merit rather than birth or privilege, our municipal identities as evidenced by our official seals became based on how we viewed ourselves. We wanted to express our identities in a more literal sense rather than through the obscure symbolism of 700-800 years of heraldic traditions developed in feudal monarchies of Europe. There, official seals were drawn and handed down from and with the approval of the government or monarchs.

One thing remains the same, though. The seal itself is official and becomes ubiquitous and can appear everywhere from welcome signs to our communities, to the podiums from which our officials speak, to identifying municipal vehicles, buildings, shoulder patches, etc. Whether the seal is based on legend or history, the original meaning is filed away, sometimes to be lost and forgotten. Some seals are self explanatory, but many are not and can be representative of a point in history that may no longer be relevant.

What I have tried to do is uncover those meanings and to celebrate the event behind the seal.

I celebrate each one as an emblem of freedom.     *Marvin Bubie*

# TREATY MAP OF 1782 (made in 1755) by John Mitchell

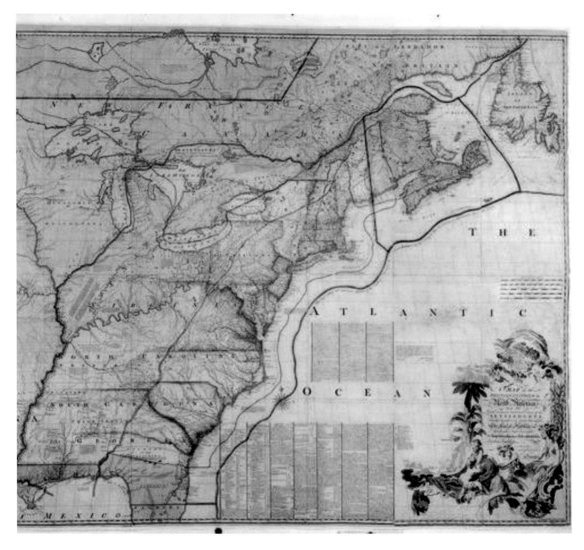

- Courtesy of Library of Congress

# CONTENTS

TEA PARTIES . . .

THE BRITISH ARE COMING . . .

MUNICIPAL SEALS / LOGOS / ETC

1620 -1774 Chapter 1

1775 Chapter 2

1776 Chapter 3

1777 Chapter 4

1778 Chapter 5

1779 Chapter 6

1780 Chapter 7

1781 Chapter 8

1782-1783 Chapter 9

ACKNOWLEDGEMENTS

RESOLVES FROM 1766 TO 1776

(Essence of)  DECLARATION of INDEPENDENCE

# THE TEA PARTIES

In September and October 1773, seven ships carrying East India Company tea were sent to the colonies: four were bound for Boston, and one each for New York, Philadelphia, and Charleston.

The closing of the Boston port was meant to intimidate the other colonies as well as punish Boston. As evidenced by the list below, it did not have the desired effect.

No tea was shipped to Newport, RI since the *Gaspee* was burned in June 1772 over the Stamp Act. These are some of the tea parties:

➢ Nov 27, 1773 - Philadelphia – British tea ship *The Polly* sent back to England with 697 chests of tea.
➢ Dec 3, 1773 – Charleston SC – *The London* offloads 257 chests of tea which is held in Old Exchange for 3 years then sold to help the Patriot cause.
➢ Dec 16, 1773 - Boston – British ship *The Dartmouth* had 342 chests of tea thrown overboard. *The Beaver* and the *Eleanor* also had another 228 chests of consigned tea dumped.
➢ Jan 16, 1774 – Princeton NJ – Tea burned in solidarity with Boston
➢ April 1, 1774 – Port of Boston closed by British Parliament as punishment for the Tea Party
➢ April 18, 1774 – New York City – *The Nancy* has 698 chests of tea destroyed by the Sons of Liberty despite the captain agreeing not to deliver it.
➢ May 23, 1774 – Chestertown MD – Tea thrown overboard from *The Geddes* and annual re-enactment features throwing a member of the Town Council overboard each year in addition to the tea.
➢ August of 1774, Norfolk VA – Citizens were shocked at the news that nine chests of tea had arrived on the brigantine *Mary and Jane.* At a meeting in the courthouse, it was collectively resolved that the tea must be sent back.
➢ Sept 15, 1774 – York ME – 150 pounds of tea stolen from storage – no tax paid.
➢ Oct 24, 1774 – Annapolis MD – 2320 lbs of tea burned and the ship *Peggy Stewart* burned as well.
➢ Oct 25, 1774 – Edenton NC – 51 women agreed to boycott English tea.

# THE TEA PARTIES

➤ Nov 3, 1774 – Charleston, SC  7 chests of tea dumped overboard from *The Brittania,* but other confiscated tea was sold for the benefit of SC

➤ Nov 7, 1774 - Yorktown VA – 2 ½ chests of tea aboard *The Virginia* on their way from England to Williamsburg were thrown overboard.

➤ Dec 22, 1774 - Greenwich NJ – Tea from the British brig *The Greyhound* that had been off loaded for secret transport to Philadelphia was discovered and burned in protest in the town square.  Center for history and New Media

➤ March 2, 1775 – Providence RI – Burned 300 lbs of tea – source Plaque placed by the societies of the Sons of the American Revolution and Daughters of the American Revolution

➤ August 26, 1776 – Fishkill NY – Tea Party – 100 women forced Abraham Brinkerhoff, Shopkeeper, to sell tea at the lawful price of six shillings per pound. – source NY State Highway Marker

There are many more examples of Tea parties.  They became a convenient form of resistance to British rule and ultimately a test of where someone's loyalties lie.

If there must be trouble, let it be in my day, that my child may have peace.
Thomas Paine, The American Crisis, No. 1, December 19, 1776

# THE BRITISH ARE COMING!

Over eight years the British held the cities and they were regularly foraging and waging war so they were always coming. There were many who warned their fellow citizens and acted in the same role as Paul Revere and were compared to him.

- ➤ December 13, 1774 – Five months before riding to Lexington, Paul Revere rode to Portsmouth NH to warn that the British were coming to take the munitions from Fort William and Mary. Patriots stormed the fort and captured the military supplies. (see Nottingham NH seal)
- ➤ April 18, 1775 – Paul Revere was joined by William Dawes and Dr. Samuel Prescott in warning the citizens in the Boston suburbs about the movement of British regulars. (see City of Revere seal)
- ➤ April 19th – an unknown horseman rides through Tewksbury MA warning that the British were coming. (see Tewksbury town seal)
- ➤ April 19th – Israel Bissill rides from Watertown MA to Philadelphia to spread the word about Lexington and Concord. The ride takes 5 days.
- ➤ December 9, 1775 – sixteen year old Betsy Dowdy rode her horse, Black Bess, over 50 miles to get the Perquimans County NC Militia's help for Patriots facing the British at Great Bridge VA.
- ➤ November 26, 1776 – In New Jersey, the "Lone Rider" rode to warn George Washington that the British had landed 200 ships and were on their way to capture what was left of his army. Although his name was not recorded, the deed is captured on the town seal of Closter NJ. (see Borough of Closter seal)
- ➤ April 26, 1777 – Sybil Ludington at 16 years old rode her horse, Star, over 40 miles in the dark to gather her father's militia to confront the British in Ridgefield CT after they had already burned the supply depot in Danbury. (see Town of Kent NY seal)
- ➤ July 5, 1779 – Teenager Thomas Painter stood watch at the Town of West Haven CT harbor entrance to warn the citizens of an impending British attack. (see City of West Haven seal)

# THE BRITISH ARE COMING!

➢ June 2, 1781 – Col Jesse Thomas was recuperating at home in Cumberland County, Virginia and learned that the British were on the way to capture the arsenal at Point of Forks.  He rode his horse, Fearnaught to warn the commander, Baron Von Steuben who was able to transport valuable stores across the James River.  Some stores were captured by the British.

➢ June 3, 1781 – Jack Jouett rode over 40 miles on his black horse, Sallie, from Richmond, Virginia to warn the Virginia Assembly and Governor Thomas Jefferson, that the British were on their way to Charlottesville to arrest them.  Again, this was accomplished through the woods and around the British patrols at night.  Jefferson escaped along with Patrick Henry, although another legislator named Daniel Boone was briefly detained by the British.

# RESOLVES, DECLARATIONS, ETC

In response to the Intolerable Acts and other acts by the British Parliament and Monarchy, there was widespread defiance in the written resolves signed by hundreds of men in hundreds of communities generally objecting to the violation of their rights as Englishmen. The declarations became stronger as the dispute escalated to outright Independence. These are just a few of those resolves.

1766 – VIRGINIA RESOLVES (VA) page 8 (see appendix)

1773 – SHEFFIELD DECLARATION (MA)

1774 – CHESTERTOWN RESOLVES (MD) (see appendix)

1774 – JAMES CITY RESOLVES (VA)

1774 – FAIRFAX RESOLVES (VA)

1774 – ORANGETOWN RESOLUTIONS (NY)

1774 – HANOVER RESOLVES (VA) (see appendix)

1774 – HUNTINGTON DECLARATION OF RIGHTS (NY)

1774 – SUFFOLK RESOLVES (SUFFOLK COUNTY MA)

1775 – FINCASTLE RESOLUTIONS (VA)

1775 – BUSH RIVER RESOLUTION (MD) page 22 (see appendix)

1775 – MECKLENBURG DECLARATIONS (NC) page 40 (see appendix)

1775 – COXSACKIE DECLARATION OF INDEPENDENCE (NY)

1775 – LIBERTY POINT RESOLVES (NC) page 49 (see appendix)

1775 – TRYON RESOLVES (NC)

1776 – HALIFAX RESOLVES (NC) page 62 (see appendix)

1776 – VIRGINIA DECLARATION OF RIGHTS

1776 – May 4th RHODE ISLAND DECLARES INDEPENDENCE

JULY 4, 1776 – DECLARATION OF INDEPENDENCE (see last page)

# 1620 - 1774

November 11, 1620 - Town of Provincetown MA

December 13, 1636 – Army National Guard

August 23, 1687 – Town of Ipswich MA

June 1755 – City of Rensselaer NY

August 11, 1759 – Town of Danvers MA

November 23, 1765 – City of Frederick MD

February 1766 – County of Westmoreland VA

June 9, 1772 – Village of Pawtuxet RI

December 16, 1773 – City of Boston MA

May 23, 1774 – Town of Chestertown MD

July 11, 1774 – City of Johnstown NY

1774 – Town of Kirkland NY

1774 – Village of Clinton NY

1774 – Town of Westmoreland NY

September 23, 1774 – City of York ME

October 24, 1774 – City of Point Pleasant WV

December 13, 1774 – City of Portsmouth NH

December 13, 1774 – Town of New Castle NH

December 14, 1774 – Town of Nottingham NH

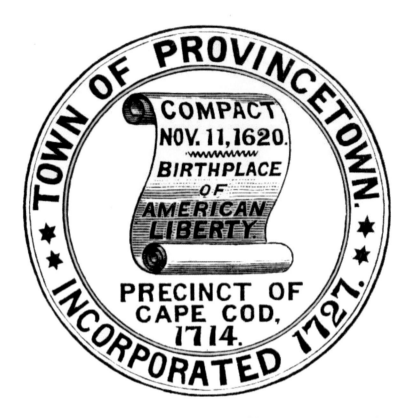

# NOVEMBER 11, 1620 -TOWN OF PROVINCETOWN MA

In 1620, the Pilgrims arrived on the Mayflower and made their first landing in the New World in Provincetown Harbor. The Pilgrims stayed in Provincetown for five weeks, where they created and signed the Mayflower Compact on Nov 11th. They then continued on to their ultimate destination of Plymouth, Massachusetts.

Among the signers were William Bradford, Myles Standish, John Alden and Priscilla Mullins. William Bradford was to become the colony's governor for 37 years. John Alden and Priscilla married and among their many descendants were two Presidents, John Adams and John Quincy Adams. Another descendant was Henry Wadsworth Longfellow. The idea of self government was initiated and signed.

The seal references the Mayflower Compact. John Adams and many historians have referred to the Mayflower Compact as the foundation of the U.S. Constitution written more than 150 years later.

*The Seal of the Town of Provincetown, Massachusetts is used with the permission from the Town of Provincetown and use of this seal does not imply endorsement of this publication in any way.*

# DECEMBER 13, 1636 – ARMY NATIONAL GUARD

When the National Guard's oldest regiments met for their first drill on the village green in Salem, Massachusetts, they were barely 3 months old, organized on December 13th, 1636, the date we now celebrate as the National Guard birthday.

The Army National Guard is the oldest component of the United States armed forces. Militia companies were formed with the first English settlement at Jamestown in 1607. The first militia regiments were organized by the General Court of the Massachusetts Bay Colony in 1636, and from the Pequot War in 1637 until the present day, the Army National Guard has participated in every war or conflict this nation has fought. The militia stood their ground at Lexington Green in 1775 when the opening shots of our War of Independence were fired.

The seal depicts the same iconic statue "Minuteman" as the one in Concord, MA

# AUGUST 23, 1687 - TOWN OF IPSWICH MA

The town became the Birthplace of American Independence when, on August 23, 1687, Ipswich citizens protested a tax that English Governor Sir Edmond Andros attempted to impose on the colony.

Ipswich residents, under the leadership of Reverend John Wise, led the protest, arguing that as Englishmen they could not abide taxation without representation. The citizens were jailed and fined for their action, but in 1689 Andros was called back to England and the Colonists received a new charter from the new sovereigns, King William and Queen Mary.

The concept of refusing taxation without representation led to the tea parties in the 1770s.

# JUNE 1758 - CITY OF RENSSELAER NY

In 1758, during the French and Indian War, the colonials dressed in buckskins, joined the British Army against the French.

The seal depicts British Army Dr. Richard Shuckburgh, sitting on a well in Fort Crailo, in Rensselaer, NY. Watching Col Thomas Fitchburg Jr. and the Connecticut Militia from Norwalk march into Albany, he wrote a derisive song about its appearance and lack of professionalism compared to the British Army. The song was Yankee Doodle Dandy. The Americans adopted the song during the Revolutionary War and played it for the British at their surrender at Saratoga and Yorktown.

Ernie Mann designed the seal based on three themes - history, legend and industry. The Half Moon dropped anchor in what is now Rensselaer in 1609. Rensselaer is also the home of Ft Crailo – the legendary home of Yankee Doodle Dandy. The locomotive symbolizes industry. Trains are still a part of Rensselaer today.

# AUGUST 11, 1759 - TOWN OF DANVERS MA

Danvers was permanently settled in 1636 as Salem Village. eventually petitioned the Crown for a charter as a town in 1757. According to legend, the King, rather than signing the charter, returned it two years later with the message "The King Unwilling."

On August 11, 1759, the town ignores the King's decree and remains a town. The seal was adopted at a town meeting in 1893 and the King's rebuff was defiantly given a place on the town's seal.                                    Peabody Institute Library

Danvers sent 5 regiments and came the futherest distance of all the towns on April 19th but suffered the most after Lexington.

# NOVEMBER 23, 1765 – CITY OF FREDERICK MD

John Thomas Schley arrived in Frederick Town in 1745 with a group of 100 settlers and built the first house here. Others quickly followed and the town prospered. From the beginning religion played a large part in the life of the town, and three churches, the Lutheran, Anglican, and Reformed (founded by Schley) were firmly established.

Through these early years there developed much unrest in the colonies over the way England was treating the people of the new lands. The first act of rebellion occurred in Frederick - the defiance of the hated Stamp Act by Twelve Immortal Judges and the hanging of the tax collector in effigy. November 23 is known as Repudiation Day in Frederick and celebrates one of the first overt acts of rebellion against Britain.

Although Frederick saw no military action during the Revolution, it did supply troops and equipment for the conflict. One notable patriot was Thomas Johnson, a good friend of George Washington, who served as Maryland's first elected governor.

*- from A Brief History by Frances A. Randall*

# FEBRUARY 27, 1766 - WESTMORELAND COUNTY VA

The seal was designed by Harry Kirk Swann of Tidwells, Westmoreland County, and adopted by the Board of Supervisors on May 12, 1971. The significance is as follows:

The quill represents those signers of the Leedstown Resolution and the Declaration of Independence who were sons of Westmoreland.

The scroll represents the Leedstown Resolutions, adopted in Westmoreland in 1766.

The Leedstown Resolutions were in opposition to the Stamp Act and were signed by 115 patriots including four of George Washington's brothers and preceded the Declaration of Independence by 10 years.

*The seal of Westmoreland County is used with the permission of the County of Westmoreland Board of Supervisors.*

## JUNE 9, 1772 - PAWTUXET VILLAGE RI

It was here in 1772 where Rhode Island patriots took the first organized military action towards independence by attacking and burning the hated British revenue schooner, *HMS Gaspee*. This was "America's First Blow for Freedom" that led directly to the establishment of permanent Committees of Correspondence, unifying the individual colonies, and starting the process of the American Revolution. We celebrate this historic role of Pawtuxet Village by playing host to the annual Gaspee Days Parade each June.

Pawtuxet means "Little Falls" in the native language, and this area was originally occupied by the members of the Sononoce Pawtuxet tribe, part of the larger Narragansett Indian nation, who used the area we know as Pawtuxet Neck as a feasting ground.

- **Source: Pawtuxet website (Pawtuxet is a part of Warwick)**

# DECEMBER 16, 1773 - CITY OF BOSTON MA

With sailing ships and a scene of the harbor including the Massachusetts State House on the seal, it is appropriate that during the Revolution, Boston is known for the Boston Tea Party. Organized by Samuel Adams and John Hancock, patriots disguised as Indians dumped tea into the harbor on December 16, 1773, triggering reprisals meant to intimidate.

The Boston Massacre also occurred here on March 5, 1770 in which Crispis Attucks was one of the first to die at the hands of British soldiers.

The seal was designed in 1822 by John Penniman, adopted in 1823 and modified in 1827. The legend "Bostonia Condita A.D. 1630" and the motto "Sicut Patribus Sit Dues Nobis" translates as "God be with us as He was with our fathers", 1 Kings, VIII, 57. At the bottom is "Civitatis Regimine Donata A.D. 1822" which means "City-Status Granted by the Authority of the State in 1822."

When displayed on the flag, there are some "buff" highlights (Continental blue, white, and buff are colors of the Revolutionary War uniforms of Boston soldiers).

# MAY 23, 1774 - TOWN OF CHESTERTOWN MD

A "tea party" occurred here with the tea being thrown overboard from *The Geddes* on May 23, 1774 in sympathy with the Boston Tea Party.

The seal was drawn by Al Grimes in conjunction with the town's 250th anniversary in 1956. The ship on the seal actually appears to be a skipjack used for oyster fishing in the Chesapeake Bay in more contemporary times. The other buildings are a part of Washington College and the town hall.

Washington College, the tenth oldest liberal arts college in the country, was founded in 1782 with the help of George Washington, who gave his name and 50 guineas in appreciation of Kent County's supplying flour to his troops, as well as the patriotic acts of our citizens during the War.

Chestertown appears to have the most fun celebrating its tea party annually on Memorial Day weekend by tossing the Tory, an unfortunate Town figure who gets "elected" with the most votes overboard with the tea.

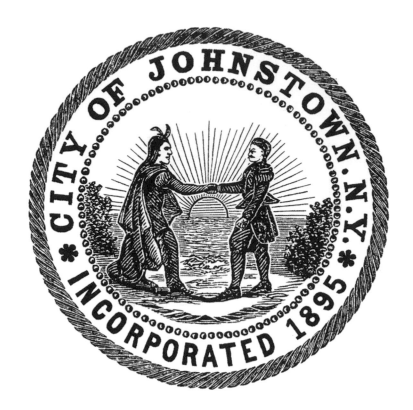

# JULY 11, 1774 - CITY OF JOHNSTOWN NY

The origin of the City of Johnstown dates back to 1763 / 1764 when Sir William Johnson was one of the controlling powers on the North American continent. He was Superintendent of Indian Affairs for the Northern Colonies of British America and was a Major General in the British Army. He received large tracts of land on the site of what are now Fulton and Hamilton Counties as a reward for distinguishing himself in the French and Indian War.

Sir William Johnson developed extremely good relations with most of the Iroquois Nation, especially the Mohawks. He died on July 11, 1774, and ultimately his heirs became Tories during the American Revolution. As a result, most of his holdings were confiscated and his heirs fled to Canada. Although the Six Nations signed an agreement in 1775 to remain neutral, in 1777 the Mohawks sided with England at the Battle of Oriskany. Some historians believe the history of the Six Nations would have been different had Johnson not died on the eve of the Revolution.

The seal depicts that friendship between Johnson and Chief Joseph Brandt who terrorized patriots in the Schoharie Valley. This eventually led to Washington's response in 1779 to defeat the Indians who had chosen to side with the British.

# TOWN of KIRKLAND
## Oneida County    State of New York

BREWERTON H. CLARKE, Sr.

**DEDICATED TO**
The Rev. Samuel Kirkland 1741-1808

# 1774 - TOWN OF KIRKLAND NY

The Town of Kirkland was first formed in 1827 from the Town of Paris.
The incorporated village, receiving its Charter on April 12, 1843, has been known as the "Village of Schools," having a total of twenty-three private schools during the nineteenth century, the most famous of which is still Hamilton College, founded by the Presbyterian missionary amongst the Oneidas, Samuel Kirkland. Hamilton College was chartered on May 22, 1812.

> (Written by Mary Bell Dever, former Historian for the Town of Kirkland)

The seal is an illustration of Rev. Samuel Kirkland with a peace pipe and a bible and was drawn by Clintonian artist Brewerton H. Clarke, Sr.

The Rev. Samuel Kirkland, for whom the Town is named was very influential with the Oneida Nation and eventually persuaded them to enter the Revolutionary War on the side of the Americans when the other Nations in the Iroquois Confederation sided with the British. Oneida Chief Skenandoa became a good friend of Rev. Kirkland and requested to be buried next to him in Clinton NY.

13

SEAL of the VILLAGE of CLINTON · NEW YORK
IN THE ORISKA VALLEY
1787

# 1774 - VILLAGE OF CLINTON NY

Moses Foote, first settler of the Village is represented with Oneida Chief Skenandoa and the Rev. Samuel Kirkland, founders of Hamilton College, against a background of hills which form the Oriska Valley and the course for the famous creek. A block of Clinton limestone carries the date of establishment, 1787. The open Bible and Calumet, carried by the great Iroquois sachem, symbolize the lasting friendship of the Indians and settlers.

The Oneidas and Tuscarora Indians sided with the Americans against the British in the Revolutionary War and suffered by the hands of the others in the Iroquois Confederacy.

Oneida Chief Skenandoa participated in the Battle of Oriskany and the Battle of Saratoga in 1777 and gained the attention of George Washington, who by some accounts named the Shenandoah Valley in Virginia for the Chief. Under Skenandoa's leadership, the Oneidas became the First Allies.

The seal was drawn by Clintonian artist, Brewerton H. Clarke, Sr.

# 1774 - TOWN OF WESTMORELAND NY

The Town of Westmoreland was the fourth town settled in the area that became Oneida County. Dean's Patent, on the Town's western line was the first area settled by James Dean, who was born in Groton, Connecticut in August 1748. He was a missionary to the Indians, mastered the Oneida tongue and was adopted by the Oneidas.

In 1774, Dean went to the Continental Congress. Representing the Indians during the Revolutionary War, Dean was stationed at Fort Stanwix and Oneida Castle. The Oneida's were induced by Mr. Dean and Mr. Kirkland, to remain neutral at the outset of the Revolution. Mr. Dean was retained in public service with the rank of Major and as agent of Indian affairs and interpreter.

In 1777 the Oneidas and the Tuscaroras joined the Patriot side while 4 other tribes sided with the British resulting in a civil war and ultimate end for the Six Nations.

# SEPTEMBER 23, 1774 - TOWN OF YORK ME

York had its own tea party on September 23, 1774, when a committee boarded the sloop "the Cynthia" and confiscated 150 lbs of English tea and placed it in a storehouse. It was later reported that a band of "Pickwacket" Indians stole the tea from the storehouse. Still later reports indicate the tea was quietly returned after the desired patriotism of York was adequately demonstrated.

The first soldiers to enter the continental army from Maine are said to have been from York. One Benjamin Simpson from this town, nineteen years of age, apprentice to a bricklayer in Boston, helped destroy the tea in the harbor.

Among the military men of the town was Johnson Moulton, who reached the rank of lieutenant-colonel. The news of the battle of Lexington reached York at evening. The inhabitants met on the following morning and enlisted a company of about sixty men, furnished them with arms, ammunition, and knapsacks full of provisions; and they marched 15 miles on the road to Boston and crossed the ferry into Portsmouth before the day closed.

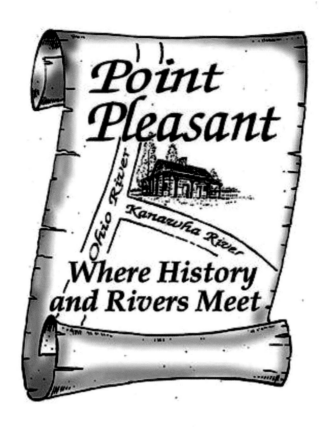

# OCTOBER 10, 1774 - CITY OF POINT PLEASANT WV

Here at the confluence of the Kanawha and Ohio Rivers, the bloody, day-long Battle of Point Pleasant was fought. Colonel Andrew Lewis' 1,100 Virginia militiamen decisively defeated a like number of Indians lead by the Shawnee Chieftain Cornstalk. A young Lt Daniel Boone was present at this battle.

Considered a landmark in frontier history, some believed the battle to be the first of the American Revolution. This action broke the power of the ancient Americans in the Ohio Valley and quelled a general Indian war on the frontier. Significantly, it also prevented an alliance between the British and Indians, one which could very possibly have caused the Revolution to have a different outcome, altering the entire history of the U.S. In addition, the ensuing peace with the Indians enabled western Virginians to return across the Allegheny Mountains to aid Revolutionary forces.

# DECEMBER 13, 1774 - CITY OF PORTSMOUTH NH

"Thus it will be seen that when Paul Revere brought his message on December 13, 1774, from the committee in Boston to Mr. Samuel Cutts of the Portsmouth committee, announcing that troops were to be sent to reinforce the fort, and bringing information, also, of the removal of the military stores in Rhode Island, and of the king's order in council prohibiting the exportation of gunpowder and military stores to America, the people were in a state of mind ready for revolt.

Certain it is that, about twelve o'clock on Wednesday, December 14, all secrecy ended; for members of the committee, accompanied by drum and fife, paraded the streets of Portsmouth and called the citizens together. By order of Governor Wentworth the chief justice of the province made proclamation that what they proposed was open rebellion against the king, but they did not waiver, and having finally gathered together a company of their townsmen, and such others as could be obtained from the adjoining towns of Newcastle and Rye, in all about four hundred men, they proceeded to Fort William and Mary. There they were warned by Captain Cochran not to enter, and were fired upon both by cannon and small arms. No one appears to have been injured, however, and they immediately stormed the fort, and easily overcame such resistance as the one officer and five effective men could offer."

*- from website*

# DECEMBER 14, 1774 - TOWN OF NEW CASTLE NH

It was on the eve of the revolution that Fort William and Mary in the Town of New Castle played its most dramatic role in history. On December 13, 1774, Paul Revere rode from Boston with a message that the fort at Rhode Island had been dismantled and troops were coming to take over Fort William and Mary. The following day the drums beat to collect the Sons of Liberty, and 400 men from Portsmouth, Rye and New Castle raided the fort and removed 98 barrels (approximately 5 tons) of gun powder.

The next night a small party led by John Sullivan stormed the fort and overcame British Captain John Cochran, and his five-man garrison carried off sixteen pieces of small cannon and military stores. This raid took place months before the incidents at Concord and is remembered as the first overt action of the American Revolution.

The gunpowder from here showed up at the Battle of Bunker Hill.

# DECEMBER 15, 1774 - TOWN OF NOTTINGHAM NH

 In October of 1774, a committee was formed to measure public interest in raising support for the 'Industrious Poor Sufferers of the Town of Boston'. At the same time, the town voted to purchase 'Two hundred weight of Good Gunpowder, lead, flints, and ten good Firelocks, as Town Stock.' The preparations for armed conflict against England had begun.

 In Portsmouth, in December of the same year, a revolutionary group known as the Committee of Safety and the Sons of Liberty plotted a raid on Fort William and Mary in New Castle. One historical account regards this attack as "the first overt act against England." Led by a Capt Pickering of Portsmouth, a force of two to three hundred colonists carried out the raid, among them several from Nottingham, in particular, Joseph Cilley and Henry Dearborn. The spoils included more than 100 barrels of gunpowder, sixteen cannon, various small arms, and other royal stores. One account has it that eight barrels of the gunpowder were brought to Nottingham and hidden in the Bartlett, Cilley and Dearborn houses on the square.

　　　　　　　- compiled by the Nottingham Historical Society from town website

The seal is the Minuteman with his musket, standing by the plow.

# 1775

March 22 - Harford County MD

March 23 - City of Richmond VA

April 18 - City of Revere MA

April 19 - Town of Tewksbury MA

April 19 - Town of Lexington MA

April 19 – Town of Boxborough MA

April 19 - Town of Norwood MA

April 19 - Town of Concord MA

April 19 - City of Nashua NH

April 19 - Town of Lincoln MA

April 19 - Town of Arlington MA

April 19 - Town of Bedford MA

April 19 - Town of Burlington MA

April 19 - Town of Acton MA

April 19 - Town of Chelmsford MA

April 19 - Town of Bloomfield CT

April 22 - City of New Haven CT

April 25 - Town of Sharon MA

May 20 – Mecklenburg County NC

June 7 – Town of Lebanon CT

June 12 – Continental Merchant Marines Created

June 14 - Continental Army Created

June 16 - Town of Marblehead MA

June 17 - Charlestown (Bunker Hill) MA

June 17 - Town of Derry NH

June 17 - Town of Dunbarton NH

June 17 – Town of Gardner MA

June 20 - Cumberland County NC

July 3 - City of Cambridge MA

July 17 – Town of Culpeper VA

July 26 - US Postal Service

September 29 – Town of Winslow ME

October 13 - Continental Navy Created

October 18 – City of Portland ME

November 10 – Continental Marines Created

November 19 - Town of Ninety-Six SC

December 9 - Culpeper County VA

# MARCH 22, 1775 - HARFORD COUNTY MD

A tablet marker located on the site of the Harford County Courts building from March 1774 until March 1783, reads …"In this house the Committee of Harford County held its meetings before and during the early years of the Revolution. Here, at a meeting held on the 22nd day of March 1775, the following members of the Committee passed and signed a formal Declaration (known as the Bush River Declaration) pledging their lives and fortunes to the cause, which, a year later, resulted in the Declaration of Independence. "

The motto "At the Risque of Our Lives and Fortunes" comprises the last eight words of the Bush Declaration and preserves the same spelling for "risk" that is used in that document. In the accepted design the shield is gold to symbolize the wealth of the county and the richness of its fields. Across the shield are waving bands of blue signifying three major county streams - Deer Creek, Bynum Run, and Winters Run. The Harford County Coat of Arms was designed by Mr. George Van Bibber and adopted by the County Commissioners on September 28, 1964.

# MARCH 23, 1775 – CITY OF RICHMOND VA

March 23, 1775 is the date of Patrick Henry's famous "Give me liberty or give me death" delivered in St. John's Church in Richmond during the Second Virginia Convention. One who heard Patrick Henry was a 15 year-old Peter Francisco who wanted to enlist on the spot. His guardian made him wait until he was 16. The speech is credited with convincing members of the House of Burgesses to pass a resolution that permitted Virginia to send troops to the American Revolutionary War. It was also a rallying cry for many Virginia soldiers including those from Culpeper.

The logo for the City of Richmond during the 1970s and 1980s was based on the statue of General George Washington at the Capitol Building.

On April 20, 1775, Royal Governor Dunmore secretly removed gunpowder from the stores in Williamsburg. Patrick Henry marched with Culpeper Militia to demand its return or compensation. On May 4th he received the compensation.

# APRIL 18, 1775 - CITY OF REVERE MA

In 1774 and the Spring of 1775 Paul Revere was employed by the Boston Committee of Correspondence and the Massachusetts Committee of Safety as an express rider to carry news, messages, and copies of resolutions as far away as New York and Philadelphia.

On the evening of April 18, 1775, Paul Revere was sent for by Dr. Joseph Warren and instructed to ride to Lexington, Massachusetts, to warn Samuel Adams and John Hancock that British troops were marching to arrest them.   After delivering his message, Revere was joined by a second rider, William Dawes, who had been sent on the same errand by a different route. Deciding on their own to continue on to Concord, Massachusetts, where weapons and supplies were hidden, Revere and Dawes were joined by a third rider, Dr. Samuel Prescott.

The seal contains a shield showing Paul Revere and the two lanterns from the Old North Church and a crescent moon with stars on a blue background.

# APRIL 19, 1775 - TOWN OF TEWKSBURY MA

"And Paul Revere was not the only man who rode. Just look at the Town Seal of Tewksbury. A rider on horseback is shown near the center of Tewksbury and the church which marked that center. The ancient tradition is that he is the person who warned the town that the British were marching." - town website

No one knows who he was. It is possible that it was he who warned Capt Cadwallader Ford of Wilmington. It is also possible that he rode on to the home of Capt Trull and then possibly to Chelmsford. And like others Capt John Trull was a man who helped spread the word that the British were out, and then marched to join the fighting. But there is even more in his case.

It is on record that a New Hampshire company of soldiers was in Cambridge after the fighting on April 19. That company had marched "and had run for over 50 miles, to do its part, and did its duty in the siege of Boston, which started that night."

# APRIL 19, 1775 - TOWN OF LEXINGTON MA

With a total population at that time of seven hundred, the town played a pivotal role in United States history when the "Skirmish on the Green" began the American Revolution. It was in Lexington, Massachusetts, on the morning of April 19, 1775, that "the first blood was spilt in the dispute with Great Britain" according to Washington's diary, when colonists faced British regulars. In this first skirmish, eight Minutemen lost their lives, ten were wounded, and two British soldiers were also wounded. After the battle, Samuel Adams exclaimed to John Hancock, "What a glorious morning for America!" It is commonly accepted that the statue on the green in town and on the seal is that of Capt John Parker.

As the British retreated back from Concord, Lexington was also the site of "Parker's revenge" as his militia ambushed them, killing several.

The annual Patriot's Day celebration in April, complete with a re-enactment of Paul Revere's ride and the battle with the British, is one of the town's most popular events.

# APRIL 19, 1775 – TOWN OF BOXBOROUGH MA

Boxborough got its name in 1783 because of its box-like shape on maps of the time. When Littleton and Acton claimed two of the town's corners as their own, the shape changed but not the name.

The fifer depicted on the town seal is said to be Luther Blanchard, who the town honors annually on the fourth Saturday each June with a Fifers Day celebration put on by local Minutemen. The Town also honors an outstanding citizen in recognition of long service to the town with the Golden Fife Award, the town's highest civic honor.

Luther Blanchard played the fife and was wounded at the Battle of Lexington.

From Town website

*. Inclusion of the Seal of the Town of Boxborough does not imply endorsement of this publication in any way.*

# APRIL 19, 1775 - TOWN OF NORWOOD, MA

The Town of Norwood, which was officially formed in 1872, was until that time part of Dedham, known as the "mother of towns," as fourteen of the present communities of eastern Massachusetts lay within its original borders.

The conflict with Britain that was to result in independence for the American colonies produced the event which more than any other, defines Norwood historically in the minds of its citizens. Captain Aaron Guild, who had served Britain earlier in its war against the French and Indians, was ploughing his fields on the morning of 19 April 1775. Upon hearing of the clash that had occurred in Lexington earlier that day, Captain Guild left plough in furrow and oxen standing and hastened to the site of the conflict, arriving in time to participate in the final stages of the battle. This legendary act is commemorated on the town seal.  This exact response was repeated dozens if not hundreds of times all over New England.

Throughout the war that began with Captain Guild's trek to Lexington, the citizens of South Dedham gave virtually total support to the revolutionary effort.

# APRIL 19, 1775 - TOWN OF CONCORD MA

As the scene of the first battle of the American Revolutionary War on April 19, 1775, it is considered the birthplace of the nation, where the "shot heard 'round the world" for liberty and self government was fired. Concord still retains many well-preserved colonial houses, nine of them on or near Concord green and witnesses of the famous Battle of Concord.

In this historic battle, which ushered in the Revolutionary War, a column of British infantry was badly mauled by colonists during a 16-mile long running battle that saw 273 British and 95 American dead.

Concord, signifying agreement and harmony, was incorporated on Sept 12, 1635.

The seal is the iconic minuteman statue by Daniel French who later sculpted the Lincoln memorial.

Note: The Seal of the Town of Concord, Massachusetts is used with permission from the Town of Concord. Inclusion of the Seal of the Town of Concord does not imply endorsement of this publication in anyway.

# APRIL 19, 1775 - CITY OF NASHUA NH

With the coming of the Revolutionary War, the men and families of Dunstable, NH, were present from the very first days of the glorious struggle. When news of the Battle of Lexington reached Dunstable by the afternoon of April 19, 1775, many men rushed to arms and hurried to Concord, MA, to participate in driving the English back to Boston. Within less than a week of the Lexington-Concord battles a company of 66 men was organized at Cambridge, MA, under Capt. William Walker of Dunstable, New Hampshire. Historian Charles Fox's History of Nashua states, "The whole man population of the town at this time between the ages of 16 and 50 was only 128; so that nearly one-half the able-bodied inhabitants must have been in the army at the first call of liberty, a month before the Battle of Bunker Hill. From no other town in New Hampshire was there so large a number in the army…"

It is a little known fact that no less than half the men who fought on Bunker Hill the day of June 17, 1775, were New Hampshire minute-men.

# APRIL 19, 1775 - TOWN OF LINCOLN MA

The Lincoln Company was the first from any of the neighboring towns to reach Concord when the fighting started. After the battle at the North Bridge, as the British retreated toward Boston, a small engagement occurred at the junction of Old Bedford Road and Virginia Road. This site was known as the Bloody Angle. Eight British soldiers were killed.

The Town Seal was adopted in 1897. At that time, Lincoln's new Town Hall (now Bemis Hall) was only five years old, and it is depicted at the base of a heraldic shield. Above it is a red cross with gold fleur-de-lis, taken from the seal of Lincoln, England. An old chestnut tree that stood on the Town Common (below Bemis Hall) is used as the crest of the shield and is symbolic of Lincoln's long-standing appreciation of its trees. Behind the shield, two crossed shepherd's crooks reflect Lincoln's agricultural heritage.

*The seal of the Town of Lincoln, Massachusetts is used with permission from the Town of Lincoln. Inclusion of the Seal of the Town of Lincoln does not imply endorsement of this publication in any way.*

# APRIL 19, 1775 - TOWN OF ARLINGTON MA

Arlington, founded over 350 years ago, remains proud of its history. The birthplace of Uncle Sam, the location of the first public children's library, and the site of most of the fighting when the British marched through it returning from the Old North Bridge at the start of the Revolutionary War, Arlington has preserved many of its historical buildings and even recreated its town common.

Battle of Menotomy (Patriot's Day): Arlington (then called Menotomy) played a prominent role on the first day of the American Revolution - April 19, 1775. Minutemen from surrounding towns converged on Menotomy to ambush the British on their retreat from Concord and Lexington. More than one-half of that fateful day's casualties were suffered in the short distance from Foot of the Rocks (at the intersection of Lowell Street and Massachusetts Avenue) to Spy Pond.

The seal highlights the Bunker Hill Monument framed by two majestic elm trees that once graced the entrance to Arlington at the Cambridge line. It was adopted in 1871. The motto translates to "The Defense of Liberty is our Ancestral Heritage."

*Inclusion of the Seal of the Town of Arlington does not imply endorsement of this publication in any way.*

## APRIL 19, 1775 – TOWN OF BEDFORD MA

The Bedford Flag is the oldest complete flag known to exist in the United States. It is celebrated as the flag carried by the Bedford Minuteman, Nathaniel Page, to the Concord Bridge on April 19, 1775, but it was already an antique on that day. It was designed in England in 1660-1710 and made for a cavalry troop of the Massachusetts Bay militia early in the colonial struggle for the continent that we call "the French and Indian Wars."

Into the rich red damask is woven a pattern of pomegranates, grapes, and leaves. The emblem consists of a mailed arm emerging from clouds and grasping a sword. Three cannonballs hang in the air. Encircling the arm is a gold ribbon on which the Latin words "VINCE AUT MORIRE" (Conquer or Die) are painted.

The town seal illustrating the flag was adopted in 1899. (Bedford Historical Society)

*Inclusion of the Seal of the Town of Bedford does not imply endorsement of this publication in any way.*

# APRIL 19, 1775 - TOWN OF BURLINGTON MA

On April 19th of 1775, British officers Lt Col Francis Smith and Major Pitcairn had specific orders to arrest the leaders of the rebellion. Their secondary goal was to capture the supplies they believed were in Concord.

Description of the seal - The text "Woburn 1642 Woburn Precinct 1730 Sewall House Incorporated Feb. 28, 1799" encircles an image of the Sewall House, the house where John Hancock, Samuel Adams and Dorothy Quincy sought refuge during the Battle of Lexington and Concord and the house that served Burlington clergy for 100 years. Built in 1730 by Benjamin Johnson, the Sewall House was destroyed by fire in 1897. The first town seal has the same elements as today's seal.

 The Town of Burlington was formed in 1799 and is sited on the watersheds of the Ipswich, Mystic and Shawsheen Rivers.

*Inclusion of the Seal of the Town of Burlington does not imply endorsement of this publication in any way.*

# APRIL 19, 1775 - TOWN OF ACTON MA

On the northwest face of the monument, directly under the arch, is cut the following inscription:

"The Commonwealth of Massachusetts and the Town of Acton, co-operating to perpetuate the fame of their glorious deeds of patriotism, have erected this monument in honor of Capt. Isaac Davis and privates Abner Hosmer and James Hayward, citizen soldiers of Acton and Provincial Minute Men, who fell in Concord Fight, the 19th day of April, A.D.1775."

"On the morning of that eventful day Provincial officers held a council of war near the Old North Bridge in Concord; and as they separated, Davis exclaimed, 'I haven't a man that is afraid to go!' and immediately marched his company from the left to the right of the line, and led in the first organized attack upon the troops of George III in that memorable war, which by the help of God, made the thirteen colonies independent of Great Britain and gave political being to the United States of America."                                        "Acton, April 19, 1851."

*Inclusion of the Seal of the Town of Lincoln does not imply endorsement of this publication in any way.*

# APRIL 19, 1775 - TOWN OF CHELMSFORD, MA

**The Revolutionary War Memorial, designed by architect Greely S. Curtis of Boston, was dedicated May 2, 1859 to the Revolutionary soldiers of Chelmsford. The memorial is twenty-seven feet tall, with a thirty-foot terrace.**

### North Side
Erected 1859
Let the children Guard
What the sires have won.

### South Side
In Honor of the Townsmen of Chelmsford
who served their Country in the
War of the Revolution
This monument is erected by a
Grateful Posterity

### East Side
Lt. Col. Moses Parker and
Capt. Benj. Walker wounded at Bunker Hill
June 17, 75 Died prisoners in Boston
July 4 & Augt. 75 Lt. Robt. Spalding
Died at Milford Ct. 76

### West Side
John Bates Died in army in Cambridge
David Spalding Jr. Died in army at Ticonderoga
Pelatiah Adams Killed at Cherry Valley
Noah Foster Shot at Capture of Burgoyne
Henry Fletcher Killed at White Plains

# APRIL 19, 1775 – TOWN OF BLOOMFIELD CT

"During the Revolutionary War, the deep staccato roll of the Brown Drum mustered the farmer and shopkeeper to arms -- and to its beat, men young and old, marched in the sacred cause of liberty -- in that historic struggle against tyranny."
*Town of Bloomfield's Bicentennial program (1976)*

Bloomfield was officially incorporated in 1835. It was originally settled in the 1600's and was a part of WINdsor which in turn became a part of Wintonbury Parish along with FarmingTON and SimsBURY. Bloomfield tradition holds that the Browns used their particular skills as coopers to produce drums that were carried in the Revolutionary War. Although there is no definitive proof that Brown Drums were in the Revolutionary War, "Bloomfield citizens celebrate the drum ...because it summons them to a high and purposeful mission."

Brown Drums are carefully guarded by museums, fife and drum corps, and historical societies. As one drummer told a reporter over 60 years ago, "A Brown drum is to a drummer what a Stradivarius is to a violinist."

# APRIL 22, 1775 – CITY OF NEW HAVEN CT

April 22 is celebrated in New Haven as Powder House Day when the Governor's Foot Guard requested the keys to the Powder House to prepare its soldiers to March into Cambridge Massachusetts marking New Haven's official participation in the American Revolution. Word of Lexington and Concord reached New Haven on the 21st and the town government had decided not to send aid to Massachusetts.

The Foot Guard (local militia led by Capt Benedict Arnold) decided overwhelmingly to support the fellow patriots in Massachusetts. A reenactment of demanding and finally receiving the keys from the First Selectman is held annually.

The original seal was drawn by Ezra Stiles and Jame Hillhouse in February 1785 and was described as having "The Devise, the Harbour of New Haven, Ship at the entrance…" The current seal contains some of the same elements.

# APRIL 26, 1775 -TOWN OF SHARON MA

Colonel Gridley assumed his assignment as Chief Engineer of the Continental Army on April 26, 1775, and was wounded at Bunker Hill. During the American Revolution, the townspeople--mostly farmers and craftsmen--made cannonballs for the Continental Army. Among the old homes surviving in the Town of Sharon since those times are the houses of the patriots Job Swift and Deborah Sampson Gannett.

The design of the seal represents a history of the Town in that the center crest, upper left quarter is an outline of Moose Hill which is the highest elevation of land between Boston and Providence, Rhode Island. The upper right quarter represents the Gun House of the Sharon Artillery Company where armor was housed for fifty years. The bottom half of the crest design represents Lake Massapoag where iron was mined from which Colonel Richard Gridley cast the first cannon made for the Revolutionary War in 1775. Above the crest there are two cannons crossed on cannonballs which represent the industry established in the Town. The belt buckle knotted at the base with 2$^{nd}$ precinct 1740 commemorates the ecclesiastical separation of the Town of Sharon from the mother Town of Stoughton. The year 1765 represents the political separation.

# MAY 20, 1775 - MECKLENBURG COUNTY NC

The Mecklenburg Declaration is the first government body to declare independence. Although there is no physical evidence of the actual document, it has been celebrated for over 100 years in the county and the state. The date is also highlighted on the NC Flag.

The banner in the eagle's claws has the date the Mecklenburg County Declaration of Independence was signed. The inkwell, quill pen, and paper also symbolize the Declaration. The farm buildings represent the county's rural or unincorporated areas, and the office buildings represent the urban or city area. The county seal also has a hornet's nest, and the two different kinds of branches represent modern and traditional times. The hornet's nest refers to the British characterization of its citizens resistance to the British Army and Loyalists later in the War.

The seal was designed by Harvey H. Boyd as a result of a contest and was adopted by the County Commissioners in October of 1964.

The Seal of Mecklenburg County is used with permission by Mecklenburg County.

# JUNE 7, 1775 - TOWN OF LEBANON CT

On June 7, 1775, the Council of Safety, authorized by the Connecticut General Assembly in response to the "Lexington Alarm," met in Jonathon Trumbull's former store which became the War Office and is depicted on the Town Seal. Governor Trumbull's leadership galvanized Connecticut's astounding contribution of men, munitions, supplies and provisions to the Continental Armies, as well as to the militia and the state's navy. This outpouring of supplies, which several times rescued Washington's troops from starvation at Valley Forge and Morristown, earned Connecticut its nickname as "The Provisions State."

Lebanon, first settled in the 1690s, was incorporated as a town in 1700. Known for its unique role in the Revolutionary War, the town became one of the most politically important towns in Connecticut. The mile-long Common is like no other green in New England. A mile in length and with a major portion still in agricultural use, the Lebanon Green is unique because of its size and its association with the American Revolution. During the Revolution, at least 677 Lebanon men served in the American units, from the Battle of Bunker Hill to the end of the campaigns in 1782, or more than 50 percent of the adult population at that time. It is these activities that earned Lebanon its place in history as "the heartbeat of the Revolution."

# JUNE 12, 1775 – US MERCHANT MARINE

On June 12, 1775, near Round Island on Machias Bay, the patriots led by Jeremiah O'Brian captured the *HMS Margaretta* in fierce hand to hand combat. News of the April 1775 battles at Concord and Lexington reached Machias, Maine, just as citizens were anxiously awaiting long-needed supplies from Boston. When the *Unity* and *Polly* carrying these supplies arrived, they were accompanied by the British armed schooner *HMS Margaretta,* under the command of Lieutenant Moore. The escort's job was to see that in exchange for supplies, lumber was taken back to Boston to build barracks for British soldiers.

The citizens refused to supply the lumber and erected a Liberty Pole instead. Lt Moore threatened to fire on the town while the citizens planned to arrest him.

This was considered the first sea engagement of the Revolution and the start of the merchant marine's war role. Letters of Marque were issued and privateering authorized.

The emblem is a contemporary design.

# JUNE 14, 1775 – UNITED STATES ARMY

The United States Army officially was created June 14, 1775, at Philadelphia, Pennsylvania. The Massachusetts Provincial Congress, aware of the necessity of enlisting the support of all of the colonies in the struggle against the British, appealed to the Continental Congress to adopt the New England army. Congress appointed a committee to draft regulations for a new Continental Army.

On June 14, Congress voted to adopt the measure, marking the official creation of the United States Army. Also, this date marks the creation of the Infantry. The same day Congress voted to raise 10 companies of riflemen. These were the first soldiers to be enlisted directly in the Continental service in Pennsylvania, Maryland and Virginia, to march north to join the current force besieging Boston.

This seal was first used during the revolution and is dated 1778. It came to be used as the seal of the Army Headquarters. The current seal contains many of the same elements.

# JUNE 16, 1775 – TOWN OF MARBLEHEAD MA

Marblehead resident Col. John Glover organized a Marblehead Militia and was officially commissioned as head of the 21st Regiment on June 16, 1775, the day before the Battle for Bunker Hill. After Glover and his Regiment fought several skirmishes on land, General George Washington and Congress commissioned Colonel Glover to lease and arm merchant vessels. Thus the claim for the birthplace of the US Navy.

In August, 1776, John Glover's Regiment evacuated Washington's Army from Long Island, in effect saving the Revolution. John Glover saved the Army again at the Battle of Pelham, fighting a successful delaying action. Men of the now-General Glover's Marblehead Regiment put their boating skills to the test again in 1776. On the evening of December 25, Glover's Regiment rowed General George Washington's Army across the stormy and treacherous waters of the Delaware River to surprise the English and Hessian troops in the Battle of Trenton.

This is the older seal which was replaced by a scene of a fisherman in 1909. It appears to be based on a design of colonial currency in Massachusetts designed by Paul Revere where the figure was holding a copy of the Magna Carta and a sword.

# JUNE 17, 1775 – CHARLESTOWN MA

On June 17, 1775, the Charlestown Peninsula was the site of the Battle of Bunker Hill. In fact, the battle actually took place on Breed's Hill, which overlooked the harbor and the town. Although the Americans ran out of ammunition and had to retreat, the British had far more casualties, and the end result was to encourage the Americans. Dr. Joseph Warren was killed at Bunker Hill. Freeman Salem Poor, who had been born a slave was recognized as a "Brave and gallant soldier" by 14 officers.

"Don't fire until you see the whites of their eyes" is attributed to Gen Israel Putnam and repeated by others including Colonel William Prescott.

The seal features the Bunker Hill Monument. The cornerstone of the Bunker Hill Monument was laid by the Marquis de Lafayette on the 50th anniversary of the battle on June 17th 1825. Construction was completed in 1843 and was dedicated by Daniel Webster.

Charlestown was annexed into Boston in 1874.

# JUNE 17, 1775 - TOWN OF DERRY NH

"During the Revolutionary War, the overwhelming majority of the townsfolk were decidedly on the side of the patriot cause. Men from our Town served first at Bunker Hill and continued on bravely to the end of the war at Yorktown. Matthew Thornton was a signer of the Declaration of Independence. General John Stark who later said "Live Free Or Die" was born here, as was General George Reid who served longer than any other Patriot leader except one - his best friend, General George Dearborn, who had enlisted one day earlier. There were a few from our town who remained loyal to the king. Foremost of these Tories was Colonel Stephen Holland who, while serving as our Selectmen, was actually a major British spy.

The seal contains an illustration of Robert Frost's Farm and an outline of New Hampshire as well as the quill for Matthew Thornton.

The town was named for the Isle of Derry, Ireland."

- from town website by Town Historian Richard Holmes

## JUNE 17, 1775 - TOWN OF DUNBARTON NH

At age 15, Caleb Stark slipped away from home on the eve of the Battle of Bunker Hill to travel to Boston and join in the Revolution. Arriving at his father's side too late to be sent back, Caleb served for the duration of the war. This adventure is depicted on the Dunbarton Town Seal. Caleb was one of the youngest Revolutionary War patriots at the Battle of Bunker Hill.

He was born December 3, 1759 at Dunbarton, New Hampshire. Caleb served with his father, General John Stark, in the 1st New Hampshire Regiment at the Battle of Bunker Hill, and later at Trenton and Princeton as an Ensign. He left the Army as a major at 24.

# JUNE 17, 1775 - TOWN OF GARDNER MA

In 1774, the area now known as Gardner, consisted of several land tracts in Ashburnham, Winchendon, Westminster and Templeton. . In 1785, a petition was written to make that area a separate Town, enough signatures were gathered and Township was granted. The Town was named for Colonel Thomas Gardner, who was fatally wounded in the Battle of Bunker Hill. Seth Heywood, one of the signers of the petition, fought alongside Col. Gardner at Bunker Hill.

SECTION 1. The seal of the City of Gardner shall be a circle two inches in diameter having in the center a representation of Col Thomas Gardner with sword in hand. In the background are Crystal Lake and Monadnock Mountain. Within the inner circle, are five small circles, the one at the top enclosing a chair, the ones on the side each enclosing the letter "W" and the one at the bottom at the left enclosing the letter "A" and the one at the bottom right enclosing the letter "T". In the margin, the inscription "Gardner, A Town June 27, 1785, a City, January 1, 1923;" the whole to be arranged according to the impression hereto annexed.

*The seal of the City of Gardner is used with the permission of the City of Gardner.*

# JUNE 20, 1775 - CUMBERLAND COUNTY NC

The Liberty Point Resolves, also known as "The Cumberland Association," was a resolution signed by fifty residents of Cumberland County, North Carolina, early in the American Revolution.

On June 20, 1775, these Patriots, who had formed themselves into a group known simply as "The Association," met to sign a document protesting the actions of Great Britain following the battles of Lexington and Concord. The signers expressed the hope that Great Britain and the colonies would be reconciled, but vowed that, if necessary, they would "go forth and be ready to sacrifice our lives and fortunes to secure her freedom and safety." The resolves were thus not a declaration of independence. Public advocation for separation from Great Britain would not become common until 1776.

The period of the American Revolution was a time of divided loyalties in Cumberland County and a considerable portion of the population, especially the Highland Scots who were staunchly loyal to the British Crown.

# JULY 3, 1775 - CITY OF CAMBRIDGE MA

July 3, 1775 – Washington assumes command of the Army under the Washington Elm.

A:  The current city seal is a revision of the original seal, which was adopted in 1846. The seal contains an image of the Gothic Revival style building, Gore Hall, the former library building at Harvard College, and an image of the Washington Elm, the Cambridge tree made famous by the popular legend of George Washington taking command of the American Army under the tree during the Revolution. The Latin motto reads: "Literis Antiquis Novis Institutis Decora."  It can be translated as: "Distinguished for Classical Learning and New Institutions."  Also written in Latin are the founding and chartering dates for the town and city, which are translated as: "Built in A.D. 1630.  Chartered a city in A.D. 1846."

The original seal of 1846 was designed by Edward Everett, the President of Harvard from 1846-1849. He also composed the Latin motto used on the seal.

# JULY 17, 1775 – TOWN OF CULPEPER VA

At the age of 17, George Washington was commissioned to survey and plot the Town and the County of Culpeper.

During the American Revolution, a group of local residents from Culpeper and the surrounding counties of Fauquier and Orange organized themselves on July 17, 1775, as the Culpeper Minute Men Battalion under a large oak tree "in Clayton's old field." Evoking the stirring words of Patrick Henry, the group rallied under a flag which depicts a rattlesnake with 13 rattles and the motto, "Liberty or Death - Don't Tread on Me."          *Culpeper Museum*

A total of 350 men were raised. One of the men from Culpeper was John Jameson, who was on duty in New York in 1778 when Maj John Andre was captured. Being suspicious of his immediate superior, Benedict Arnold, he instead reported the incident directly to George Washington. He helped to foil the plot to turn West Point over to the British. This plot was the most notorious act of treason in the country.

# JULY 26, 1775 – US POSTAL SERVICE

After the Boston riots in September 1774, the colonies began to separate from the mother country. A Continental Congress was organized at Philadelphia in May 1775 to establish an independent government. One of the first questions before the delegates was how to convey and deliver the mail.

Benjamin Franklin, newly returned from England, was appointed chairman of a Committee of Investigation to establish a postal system. On July 26, 1775, Franklin was appointed Postmaster General, the first appointed under the Continental Congress. The establishment of the organization that was to become the United States Postal Service nearly two centuries later traces back to this date.

Benjamin Franklin was one of the oldest and perhaps the wisest, most respected of our founding fathers and had been appointed a postmaster for the Crown in 1753 prior to the Revolution. He was an obvious choice for the critical position of establishing the postal service for the emerging nation.

This was the original seal for the Post Office Department.

# SEPTEMBER 29, 1775 - TOWN OF WINSLOW ME

In 1775, the new Continental Army initiated its first major offensive – the invasion of Canada. From Cambridge, MA, Col. Benedict Arnold followed the Kennebec River north, stopping at Fort Halifax in Winslow on his ill-fated attempt to invade Canada in September 1775. The rugged Maine wilderness caused 300 of the 1,100 to turn back and an additional 200 died enroute. The entire offensive ultimately failed.

In 1754-5 a fortification was erected by Governor Shirley at the junction of the Sebasticook with the Kennebec as an outpost, which was named Fort Halifax. A single block-house of this fort is still standing a little to the north of the bridge over the Sebasticook and may be seen from the cars, looking toward the Kennebec. The town was incorporated in 1771, being named in honor of General John Winslow, who had command of the force employed in the erection of Fort Halifax.

Fort Halifax in Winslow, Maine, is a National Historic Landmark and the oldest blockhouse in the United States.

# OCTOBER 13, 1775 – UNITED STATES NAVY

"On Friday, October 13, 1775, meeting in Philadelphia, the Continental Congress voted to fit out two sailing vessels, armed with ten carriage guns, as well as swivel guns, and manned by crews of eighty, and to send them out on a cruise of three months to intercept transports carrying munitions and stores to the British army in America."

This was the original legislation out of which the Continental Navy grew and as such constitutes the birth certificate of the navy.

The seal is on a circular background, with a three masted square rigged ship underway, supported by a stylized sea scroll, over an inclined anchor. Below the anchor is a scroll with the Latin words SUSTENTANS ET SUSTENTATUM, which means "sustaining and having sustained," or "upholding and having upheld." The inscription around the edge is USA SIGIL. NAVAL at the top and thirteen stars around the bottom. This is known as the Admiralty seal and is no longer used.

# OCTOBER 18, 1775 – CITY OF PORTLAND ME

The city seal depicts a phoenix rising out of ashes, which goes with its motto, Resurgam, Latin for "I will rise again," in reference to Portland's recoveries from four devastating fires.

On October 18th, 1775, in the midst of the Revolutionary War, the British Navy under the command of Captain Henry Mowat brought the city to its knees once more in its struggle for stability. This may have been in retaliation for the Battle of Machais earlier in the year.

Portland has earned the right to use the Phoenix rising from the ashes as its city seal. The seal alludes to the city's numerous rebirths; first following Indian raids in the 17th century, again following bombardment by the English navy during the American Revolution, and most significantly, following a massive fire that was the unfortunate conclusion to a July 4th celebration in 1866. The consequence of the fire is evident in Portland's architecture – which is largely brick, often Victorian and mostly dating from the last 150  years.

## JOURNAL OF THE CONTINENTIAL CONGRESS
(Philadelphia) Friday, November 10, 1775

"Resolved, That two Battalions of marines be raised, consisting of one Colonel, two Lieutenant Colonels, two Majors, and other officers as usual in other regiments; and that they consist of an equal number of privates with other battalions; that particular care be taken, that no persons be appointed to office, or enlisted into said Battalions, but such as are good seamen, or so acquainted with maritime affairs as to be able to serve to advantage by sea when required; that they be enlisted and commissioned to serve for and during the present war between Great Britain and the colonies, unless dismissed by order of Congress: that they be distinguished by the names of the first and second battalions of American Marines, and that they be considered as part of the number which the continental Army before Boston is ordered to consist of."

Although the emblem has undergone inevitable changes over time, it has always included a "fouled anchor" (with one or more turns of chains around it). Its roots go back to the Continental Marines and the British Royal Marines. Our emblem shows an American Eagle instead of a crown and the Western Hemisphere instead of the Eastern Hemisphere on the globe.

November 10, 1775 is considered the birthday of the US Marines.

# NOVEMBER 19, 1775 - TOWN OF NINETY SIX SC

The first land battle of the Revolutionary War in the South was fought at Ninety Six on November 19-21, 1775. About 500 Patriots hastily built a rustic fort of fence and rails and bales of straw, dug a well inside and fought an attack from a much larger force of Tories. There were casualties on both sides, the first blood shed for American independence in this region. The battle ended in a formal truce.

Considered a key backcountry outpost, British forces later fortified Ninety Six, building a stockade around the village and at one corner constructing a star-shaped fort of massive earthen embankments. Inside Star Fort, the British held out for 28 days in May through June 1781 against a siege by General Nathanael Greene and his American Continental Army. The Americans started a tunnel through which they planned to blow up Star Fort, but the Redcoats under Lord Rawdon marched from Charleston to aid the garrison, and General Greene had to withdraw before superior numbers.

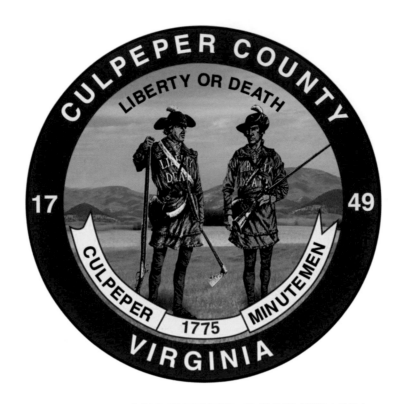

# DECEMBER 9, 1775 – CULPEPER COUNTY VA

In 1775 the Virginia Convention in Richmond divided the colony into sixteen districts and instructed each district to raise a battalion of men "to march at a minute's notice."  The Culpeper Minutemen flag is inscribed with the words, "Liberty or Death," hence the center of the Culpeper County seal is designed to highlight the Minutemen and the slogan.  Among the Culpeper Minuteman was John Marshall, future Chief Justice of the US and his father, Col Thomas Marshall.

The Culpeper Minutemen were represented at the Battle of Great Bridge (present City of Chesapeake) on December 9, 1775, where the British and Loyalists under Lord Dunsmore lost over 100 men killed and wounded vs. 1 patriot wounded. As a result of this battle, the British abandoned their plans to defeat the Americans in Virginia and decided to concentrate their forces in the North.

*The seal of Culpeper County is used with permission of the County of Culpeper.*

# 1776

Jan 1 – City of Somerville MA

Jan 26 – Town of Woodstock VA

Apr 12 – Halifax County NC

Apr 22 – Cumberland County VA

Apr – City of Washington NC

May 27 – Town of Salisbury CT

Jun 9 – Mathews County VA

Jun 17 – Village of Whitehall NY

Jun 28 – Town of Sullivan's Island SC

Jun 29 – Borough of Wildwood Crest NJ

Jul 4 – City of Philadelphia PA

Jul 5 – Commonwealth of Virginia

Jul 5 – Borough of Paulsboro NJ

July – Town of Kingston MA

Aug 2 – Borough of Roselle NJ

Aug 2 – Gwinnett County GA

Aug 27 – Town of Huntington NY

Sep 22 – Town of Coventry CT

Sep 22 – Town of E Haddam CT

Oct 18 – Town of Pelham NY

Oct 28 – City of White Plains NY

Oct 28 – Town of North Castle NY

Nov 16 – Borough of Ft Lee NJ

Nov 20 – Borough of Closter NJ

Nov 20 – Borough of Little Ferry NJ

Nov 20 – City of Englewood NJ

Nov 20 – Borough of River Edge NJ

Nov 20 – City of Hackensack NJ

Dec 25 – Township of Hopewell NJ

Dec 26 – Township of Ewing NJ

Dec 26 – City of Trenton NJ

# JANUARY 1, 1776 - CITY OF SOMERVILLE MA

As a part of Charlestown, areas existing in modern-day Somerville were critical military positions in the American Revolution. The historic Powder House - now considered one of the most distinct ancient ruins in Massachusetts - housed gunpowder for Revolutionary soldiers during the war. During the British invasion, Somerville (Charlestown) was part of the route ridden by Paul Revere on his famous "Midnight Ride." Finally, and most notably, Prospect Hill was the site of the raising of the first Grand Union Flag, under the orders of General George Washington, on January 1, 1776.

The City raises a replica of the First Flag of the Great Union each year, representing the thirteen original colonies of the United States of America. The Program also includes songs, readings, and the Post 19 Guard leading a gun salute as the Flag is raised atop the Tower on Prospect Hill.

WOODSTOCK, VIRGINIA
A TIME TO PRAY — A TIME TO FIGHT
PETER MUHLENBERG
FOUNDED 1752

## JANUARY 21, 1776 - TOWN OF WOODSTOCK VA

Woodstock's historical zenith was probably reached on January 21, 1776, in a church in the center of town when the pastor Peter Muhlenberg preached a dramatic call to arms and organized the nucleus of the 8th Virginia Regiment on the spot.

The seal depicts the famous incident when Peter Muhlenberg took off his clerical robes to reveal the uniform of a soldier. Reverend Muhlenberg took his sermon text from the third chapter of Ecclesiastes, which starts with *"To every thing there is a season..."* after reading the eighth verse, *"a time of war, and a time of peace,"* he declared, "And this is the time of war," removing his clerical robe to reveal his Colonel's uniform.

"A TIME TO PRAY – A TIME TO FIGHT" is incorporated in the design.

## APRIL 12, 1776 – HALIFAX COUNTY NC

Halifax County's rich history sets it apart. April 12, 1776, the date commemorated on the North Carolina flag, signifies the Fourth Provincial Congress' adoption of the Halifax Resolves during a meeting right here in Halifax. With that action, North Carolina became the first colony to take a bold, official step toward declaring independence from England. You can step back in time in Historic Halifax and experience the lifestyle of those early revolutionaries.

Established in 1758, Halifax County is in northeastern North Carolina, eight miles from the Virginia border.

The Historic Halifax Visitor's Center offers a museum, brief film, living history demonstrations, and tours of ten historic structures and a unique archaeological exhibit.

# APRIL 22, 1776 – COUNTY OF CUMBERLAND VA

Settlement of what is now known as Cumberland County dates to as early as 1723 when Thomas Randolph recorded a patent for 2870 acres on the Willis Creek. Along the main roads there developed a series of taverns offering travelers food, commodities, shelter, and social life. These taverns became the nuclei for the first communities in Cumberland County.

One of these taverns was Effingham, located across from the Cumberland Courthouse building. At Effingham in Cumberland Courthouse, Carter Henry Harrison read one of the first calls for the independence in the colonies on April 22, 1776. John Mayo and William Fleming subsequently presented this statement to the Virginia Convention. This initial call for independence, soon joined by other voices, led to the Declaration of Independence. George Walton, born in Cumberland County, signed this seminal document in the history of the United States.

Source: Cumberland County Comprehensive Plan 2006-2011, August 2006, Cumberland County

The seal depicts a Revolutionary soldier or Minuteman.

# 1776 - CITY OF WASHINGTON NC

Before he was President and before he won a victory, Col James Bonner named a new town after Gen Washington whom he had served under. The settlement that would be called Washington appeared in the 1770s when James Bonner started a town on his farm which bordered the Pamlico and Tar Rivers. First called Forks of the Tar, the name was changed in 1776 to Washington in honor of General George Washington, making it the Original Washington.

Washington played a strategic role during the War for Independence. With the ports of Savannah, Charles Town, and Wilmington under British siege, the Continental Army relied on Washington as a supply port. After the war, the town grew in importance as a commercial and cultural center due to its prized location on navigable waterways. Washington soon established itself as the economic center of Beaufort County and its agriculture, fishing, and commerce trades.

The seal contains elements of the Washington family coat of arms and refers to its claim of being the first municipality named after Washington.

# MAY 27, 1776 – TOWN OF SALISBURY CT

Salisbury Connecticut is justifiably proud of its slogan the "Arsenal of the Revolution" because of the cannon that were produced there during the years of the Revolutionary War. The first pour producing cannon occurred on May 27, 1776. Ironmaster Samuel Forbes and his men went on to produce over 850 cannon during the Revolutionary War along with several thousand cannon balls and other implements needed by Washington's army. These cannon ranged in size from four pounders to fourteen pounders and were used on both land and sea. It has been estimated by historians that the Salisbury furnace produced 42% of all the cannon used in Washington's army. Were it not for these cannon there is no doubt that the colonists would have lost the war and we would still be subjects of the British Crown.

The design of the seal was created by John A. Wedda, member of the Board of Selectman. It was adopted on October 22, 1964. The Town seal was adapted from the Seal of Salisbury, England. At the top is the Eagle, the emblem of the United States; the stone arch is the main structure of the colonial iron furnace; Weatogue was the Indian name meaning Wigwam Place; the crossed cannon and cannon balls recognize our pre-eminence in supplying ordnance for the army of the Revolution.

- source: Salisbury Cannon Museum brochure

# JUNE 9, 1776 - MATHEWS COUNTY VA

In 1773, Lord Dunmore, the last colonial governor of Virginia, established a stronghold on the County's Gwynn Island. Following an engagement with General Andrew Lewis at Cricket Hill in Mathews County on June 9, 1776, Lord Dunmore was forced to leave Virginia and return to England.

The Continental Navy built many of its ships in the county during the Revolution.

Mathews County is located on the eastern tip of Virginia's Middle Peninsula, which is formed by the Rappahannock River, the York River and the Chesapeake Bay.

The county is noted for its history. Mathews County was named for Brigadier General Thomas Mathews in 1791 who was then speaker of the House of Delegates of the General Assembly of Virginia.

The Mathews County seal was adopted on February 11, 1793 and symbolizes the shipbuilding industry, which was of major importance to the economy of the county.

**Village of Whitehall**

*Birthplace of the United States Navy*

*Settled 1759*

## JUNE 17, 1776 - VILLAGE OF WHITEHALL NY

The American Revolution was in its infancy when the Continental Congress gave orders *"to build, with all expedition, as many gallies and armed vessels as ... shall be sufficient to make us indisputably masters of the lakes Champlain and George."* (Journal of the Continental Congress, June 17, 1776)

Brig Gen Benedict Arnold's flagship was initially the USS Royal Savage, a 2-masted schooner, but he transferred to the USS Congress, a row galley. Arnold's fleet included the USS Revenge and USS Liberty, also schooners, as well as the USS Enterprise, a sloop, and 8 gondolas: USS New Haven, USS Providence, USS Boston, USS Spitfire, USS Philadelphia, USS Connecticut, USS Jersey, USS New York, and the galley USS Trumbull. Of the 700 Americans who began the battle for control of Lake Champlain, over 70 were killed or wounded and 100 captured.

The British defeated Benedict Arnold, but the activity effectively delayed the British from launching an attack until the following year, giving the Americans additional time for preparations and the eventual defeat of Burgoyne at Saratoga.

# JUNE 28, 1776 - TOWN OF SULLIVAN'S ISLAND SC

Carolina Day celebrates the American victory at the Battle of Sullivan's Island on June 28, 1776.

Colonel William Moultrie commanded Fort Sullivan on that fateful day when, despite being outnumbered, he and the Second South Carolina Regiment repelled assaults by the Royal Navy and the British Army. The palmetto logs used in the construction of the fort proved to be remarkably spongy and deflected the cannon balls. The battle was commemorated by the addition of a white palmetto tree to the flag of South Carolina.

The seal depicts Sgt William Jasper who retrieved the Regimental flag after the flagstaff had been shot away. While still exposed to fire, he affixed the flag to a parapet of the fort using a cannon sponge staff. Behind him is an illustration of a sailing ship assumed to be a British warship.

The Town was incorporated in 1817 as Moultrieville and became the Town of Sullivan's Island in 1906.

# JUNE 29, 1776 - BOROUGH OF WILDWOOD CREST NJ

The Battle of Turtle Gut Inlet is a documented naval encounter. On the 28th of June, 1776, the brigantine Nancy was sighted off the coast of Cape May. She was bound from the Virgin Islands with a cargo of urgently needed munitions for the Continental Army. An urgent message was sent to Captain John Barry of the Continental frigate Lexington that two British warships were already pursuing her. The Lexington set out to aid the Nancy anchoring near Cape May to wait out the night. At first light Barry's men assisted in removing the cargo from the brig which had grounded. Though only about two-thirds of gunpowder had been unloaded, Captain Barry ordered the men to abandon the Nancy, but not without leaving a calling card for the British. He ordered about fifty pounds of gunpowder to be poured in the ship's mainsail and wrapped as tightly as possible.

The British sailors who reached the Nancy raised a cheer of victory as they climbed aboard, but at that moment the gunpowder exploded with a roar that was heard forty miles above Philadlphia. The enemy ships retreated and the precious gunpowder was sent safely up the Delaware Bay. By 1794 Captain Barry would be known as Commodore Barry, "the father of the American Navy." - www.cresthistory.org

# JULY 4, 1776 - CITY OF PHILADELPHIA PA

Many events occurred in Philadelphia during the Revolution and particularly the events leading up to the War.  The British occupied the city in 1777-78.

The single most important is the Declaration of Independence on July 4, 1776.

By 1789, the Revolution had changed the status of everything and a new seal was adopted.  The shield in the center was divided into three horizontal compartments - the upper containing a plow with bare hand at one end, an imageless panel in the middle, and a ship in full sail in the lower.  Around the outer edge are the words "The Seal Of The City Of Philadelphia."   The current seal dates from 1874.

★ ★ ★ ★ ★ ★ ★ ★ ★ ★ ★ ★ ★ ★ ★ ★

On July 9th George Washington has the Declaration read to the troops in New York City.

On September 9th Congress gave that new Nation a name, calling it the "United States."

# JULY 5, 1776 – COMMONWEALTH OF VIRGINIA

Virginia's great seal was adopted by the Virginia Convention on July 5, 1776. Its design was the work of a committee chaired by George Mason, who was the principal author of the Virginia Declaration of Rights and the first Virginia Constitution. George Wythe, Richard Henry Lee, and Robert Carter Nicholas also served as members of the committee. Taking its theme from ancient Roman mythology, the seal emphasizes the importance of civic virtue.

The committee did not want a design in the style of coats-of-arms used in Britain. They did have a strong admiration for the Roman Republic and designed the new seal around the mythology of Ancient Rome.

Note: this is the first seal adopted after the Declaration of Independence and served notice that we would not be bound by rules of European heraldry. It also served notice to King George III that we would not tolerate his tyranny even in the "Old Dominion" once considered the most faithful of colonies.

# JULY 5, 1776 – BOROUGH OF PAULSBORO NJ

On July 5, 1776, Margarett Paul, widow of John Paul and her son, Benjamin Weatherby, sold 96 acres of Billingsport for 600 pounds of Pennsylvania currency to the Council of Safety of Philadelphia. The land was charged to Congress. This was the first piece of land bought by our federal government.

In 1777 a redoubt and fort were erected at Billingsport by troops from Virginia, Pennsylvania, South Carolina, and New Jersey in accordance with plans prepared by the Polish patriot Kosciuszko. Part of a defense system established for the lower Delaware River, the purpose of this fort was to build and maintain the chevaux-de-frise on the river to prevent the entrance of the British to Philadelphia. The chevaux-de-frise were made of poles from 30-40 feet in length. On the point of each stick was fastened a long, sharp piece of iron for piercing the bottom of any vessel which passed over it.

On August 1, 1777, the fort was inspected by General Washington and the Marquis de Lafayette and the men were commended by them for their work.

# JULY 1776 - TOWN OF KINGSTON MA

On August 8, 1950, The Board of Selectmen formally approved the Seal for the Town of Kingston.

The Seal was designed and drawn by Helen Foster, a native of Kingston, and a direct descendent of Francis Cook, who came over on the Mayflower. Its design was based on the early shipbuilding industry, which flourished along the banks of the Jones River in Kingston. Ms. Foster, one of the first recognized female commercial artists in Boston, illustrated the design with the *Brig Independence*, built in Kingston. The Brig's anchors were forged at the New Forge on the Forge Pond privilege off the Jones River. The *Brig* is encircled within a rope formed at the Cordage Company in North Plymouth.

The anchor, which is part of the Seal design, is representative of the smelting of abundant, native iron ore found along the bogs of the Jones River and its tributaries. Mills and foundries developed as early industries in Kingston. Iron ore was processed into tacks, nails, augers, stives, shovels, spades and anchors. Kingston anchors were known far and wide.     - TOWN OF KINGSTON WEBSITE

# AUGUST 2, 1776 - BOROUGH OF ROSELLE NJ

Born February 15, 1726, Abraham Clark was the great-grandson of Richard Clark, who came here from Long Island in 1678, and the family later acquired farmland in the present Roselle area. Not considered strong enough for farm labor, Abraham took up the study of law, and became the High Sheriff of Essex County, as his father had been earlier. Although never formally educated as a lawyer, he was called upon to settle many disputes, and became known as "the poor man's counselor."

Well respected by his neighbors, he was sent by them to the First and then the Second Continental Congress, where he voted for and signed the Declaration of Independence. Later he was a member of the Annapolis Convention, which established the need for the 1787 Constitutional Convention. He and other heroes of the Revolutionary War are buried in some of the oldest cemeteries in Union County.

Most signatures of the Declaration of Independence occurred on August 2, 1776, with the remaining occurring later.

# AUGUST 2, 1776 - GWINNETT COUNTY GA

Gwinnett County is named after Button Gwinnett, signer of the Declaration of Independence. Although the Declaration was adopted on July 4th, most members did not sign it until August 2, 1776.

The central illustration is a scroll with a quill to honor Button Gwinnett. There are thirteen rays for the original 13 colonies. The banner contains the date the county was founded. The cotton bales represent the county's early agriculture, the trees represent a green heritage to be preserved and the modern buildings represent growth.

The Gwinnett seal was adopted by the Board of Commissioners on June 7, 1988. It was drawn by Mr. Bill Prendergast, a local artist.

# AUGUST 27, 1776 - TOWN OF HUNTINGTON NY

In June 1774 Huntington adopted a "Declaration of Rights" affirming "that every freemans property is absolutely his own" and that taxation without representation is a violation of the rights of British subjects. The Declaration of Rights also called for the colonies to unite in a refusal to do business with Great Britain. Two years later news of the Declaration of Independence was received with great enthusiasm in Huntington, but the euphoria was short-lived. This event is celebrated annually.

Following the defeat of the rebel forces at the Battle of Long Island on August 27, 1776, Long Island was occupied by the British Army. Residents were required to take oaths of allegiance to the Crown. If a man refused to take the oath, he and his family could be turned off their property, losing everything. In 1782 the occupying army established an encampment in Huntington's Old Burying Ground, razing tombstones to clear the site. Not surprisingly, many townspeople resisted, waging guerilla warfare until the war was over and the British left in 1783.

Nathan Hale landed at Huntington in 1776, coming by boat from Norwalk, Connecticut. A memorial stands at the approximate site of his coming ashore in Huntington, an area now known as Halesite. Source: Town website

*SEAL of COVENTRY CONNECTICUT*

*INCORPORATED — 1712*

NATHAN
1755

HALE
1776

## SEPTEMBER 22, 1776 - TOWN OF COVENTRY CT

Nathan Hale went "under cover" for General George Washington and was caught by the British on Long Island, and summarily hanged as a spy on 22 September 1776. Nathan was 21 years old. A graduate of Yale, Capt Hale gave a speech before his execution, one line of which has been engraved on the hearts of many American Patriots: *"My only regret is that I have but one life to lose for my country!"*

Coventry is the birthplace of Nathan Hale, whose patriotism during the American Revolution distinguishes him as Connecticut's official State Hero. Visitors from around the world enjoy the Nathan Hale Homestead, an operating museum on the history of the Hale Family. Coventry is the home of the Nathan Hale Ancient Fife & Drums, which performs throughout the East Coast and holds a Colonial Encampment and Muster at the Hale Homestead each July. Other annual events held at the Homestead include Capt Hale's birthday party, walking tours, lantern tours, and corn maze adventure.

# SEPTEMBER 22, 1776 – TOWN OF EAST HADDAM CT

The school house where Nathan Hale taught during the winter of 1773-1774 was originally built in 1750 located in East Haddam Village near what is now the Nathan Hale Green.  The building was moved from Goodspeed Plaza to its present location on a hill overlooking East Haddam Village and the Connecticut River.

Owned by the Sons of the American Revolution, the schoolhouse has displays of Nathan Hale's possessions and items of local history. During the winter months, eagles can be seen perched in the tall pine trees on the schoolhouse grounds.  The schoolhouse is open May through October on Wednesday through Sunday (and Holidays) from noon to 4:00pm or by appointment.

Over 350 men served during the period of the Revolutionary War with many notable East Haddamites involved in the efforts.

The seal contains an illustration of the Nathan Hale School House.

# OCTOBER 18, 1776 - THE BATTLE OF PELHAM NY

The Battle of Pelham was fought along Split Rock Road on October 18, 1776. No part of the battle is known to have taken place inside what is today's Village of Pelham. The Village of Pelham, however, was closely connected with the aftermath of the Battle.

The Battle of Pelham is widely agreed to have saved Washington's army. Sir William Howe, Commander of the British forces, hoped to use ships moving up Long Island Sound to land troops who would race across the mainland and cut off Washington's army pulling back from the northern end of Manhattan and the area around King's Bridge in today's Bronx toward White Plains. In effect, Sir Howe hoped to flank Washington's entire army and, at a minimum, interrupt the flow of supplies to the American army from New England. The Battle of Pelham destroyed Howe's plans.

Col John Glover was given the task of delaying the British. His 700 soldiers effectively delayed over 4000 of the enemy from advancing while the rest of the army continued its retreat.

## OCTOBER 28, 1776 - CITY OF WHITE PLAINS NY

The Battle of White Plains took place on October 28, 1776. The events leading up to the Battle of White Plains flowed from the British defeat of Washington's troops in the Battle of Long Island that previous summer.

To early traders it was known as "the White Plains," either from the groves of white balsam which are said to have covered it, or from the heavy mist that local tradition suggests hovered over the swamplands near the Bronx River. The first non-native settlement came in November 1683, when a party of Puritans from Connecticut moved westward.

The seal depicts the battle flag of the rebels as well as the date of the first settlement of the White Plains area, the date of the battle – 1776 and the date of the city charter.

# OCTOBER 28, 1776 - TOWN OF NORTH CASTLE

During the Revolution, North Castle was officially considered neutral territory, though it was strongly patriotic. During the Battle of White Plains, General Washington had men positioned high in North Castle's hills. Examples of protective earthworks can still be seen at Miller Hill, where Washington's men fired down at the British troops of General Howe, holding them from advancing.

Excerpt from the Town Board minutes of January 2, 1967:
Councilman Lander reported that he, together with Frank Foster, have, after a year's study and work, prepared a new Town seal as outlined and impressed below; that in conformity with the previous actions of the Town Board, this new official North Castle seal illustrates (top left) the Town's participation in the American Revolution; (top right) the corn, wheat and potatoes that were once North Castle's agricultural staples; …….. The new seal replaces a plain one designed by William H. Creemer, Town Clerk in 1879.

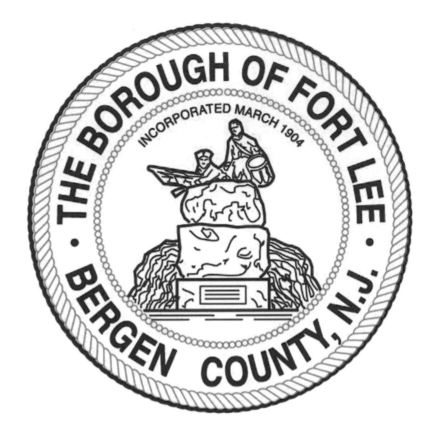

# NOVEMBER 16, 1776 - BOROUGH OF FORT LEE NJ

Fort Lee found its place in American history during the 1776 British campaign to control New York City and the Hudson River. After the siege of Boston, Washington turned his attention to the defense of New York and the Hudson Valley. The British plan was to control the length of the Hudson with the overwhelming dominance of its Royal Navy. The plan, if successful, would split the colonies in half and hopefully bring an early end to the Revolution.

The Tablet on the Rock in Monument Park dedicated on November 20, 2001 reads:

"225 years ago patriot Thomas Paine wrote about his experience in Fort Lee in "The Crisis". He spoke of "summer soldiers" and "sunshine patriots". Those were the times that tried men's souls. At that, the darkest hour of our American Revolution, Paine, General Washington and the troops of the American Army turned Retreat into Victory. The retreat road out of Fort Lee led to the establishment of our America. The world was turned upside down by those brave patriots. We rededicate this monument to their cause, American Liberty."

# NOVEMBER 20, 1776 - BOROUGH OF CLOSTER NJ

The lands which later came to be the Village of Closter played a key role in the fight for independence during the Revolutionary days. The British were entrenched in New York City, and Washington's troops were in the Hudson Highlands. Although no major battles were fought in Closter, it was a scene of numerous foraging raids by both the British and Continental armies.

A monument on Piermont Road recalls the farmer on his plow horse as the unknown Lone Horseman who is credited with warning General Greene at Fort Lee that the British were coming. When Lord Cornwallis landed at Closter Dock with 200 ships and thousands of troops on November 20, 1776, climbed the Palisades and headed South, the soldiers at Fort Lee had already moved on to Hackensack. This event is commemorated by the Lone Horseman depicted on the Closter Borough seal designed by artist Marcel Jovine.

The Lone Horseman is the Paul Revere of Bergen County.

# NOVEMBER 20, 1776 - BOROUGH OF LITTLE FERRY NJ

Incorporated in 1894, the Borough was named after the rope-drawn Little Ferry that crossed the Hackensack River between 1659 and 1826.

The Ferry played an important part in the revolution. It was used on November 20, 1776, by a detachment of Washington's troops who were fleeing the advancing British Army. The troops marched up what is now Washington Avenue and Liberty Street into Hackensack to join the other troops.

The seal depicts the rope drawn ferry with a horse and wagon reflecting the historical nature of Little Ferry.

- information provided by the Borough of Little Ferry and used by the permission of the Governing Body of Little Ferry

# NOVEMBER 20, 1776 - CITY OF ENGLEWOOD NJ

Although no major battles were fought here, events vital to the American cause did occur in Englewood.  On the night of November 20, 1776, the British General Lord Cornwallis crossed the Hudson with nine thousand men to what is now Alpine, planning to capture the rebel forces at Fort Lee, under Nathanael Greene.  General Washington, alerted to the plan, led his army from Fort Lee, down the King's Highway to the Liberty Pole Tavern, and cut over on what is now Teaneck Road to New Bridge (River Edge), where he was able to cross the Hackensack.

This area was named for a Liberty Pole erected here before the Revolution. The strategic junction was the scene of many American and British troop movements, including the 1776 retreat of the Continental Army from Fort Lee, and British activity in 1776 and 1778.  Contemporary reports suggest that the Americans passed through Liberty Pole just minutes before Cornwallis arrived, coming down Tenafly Road. Instead of pursuing Washington, Cornwallis went on to Fort Lee to seize goods stored there. Washington's army escaped to safety.

# NOVEMBER 20, 1776 – BOROUGH OF RIVER EDGE NJ

Considerable military activity occurred in River Edge throughout the Revolution. Surprised by the British invasion on November 20, 1776, General Washington led the retreating garrison from Fort Lee across the New Bridge to safety, inspiring Thomas Paine's memorable refrain, "These are the times that try men's souls."

The British failure to capture the American garrison at Fort Lee, and perhaps defeat the American rebellion, was a consequence of self-confident British officers not realizing, despite reminders from local Loyalists, that "New Bridge was the key to the peninsula between the Hackensack and the Hudson."

The seal was designed by John S. Carnes and adopted in 1957. The color aquamarine, anchor and rope border symbolize the role of the Hackensack River to the town. The plow symbolizes the farm heritage and the musket symbolizes the role that was played in the Revolutionary War.

# NOVEMBER 20, 1776 - CITY OF HACKENSACK NJ

Washington received word of the landing at 10 A.M. while at Hackensack. The British were only 11 miles away from Fort Lee, but the first half mile contained the obstacle of the precipice of the Palisades. Washington's headquarters at Hackensack was six miles from the fort. The route of the advancing troops met the route of the retreating Americans from the fort at Liberty Pole Tavern. Some reports have the British missing the Americans within hours.

About noon on November 22nd, the British took possession of Hackensack, and in the afternoon the Green was covered with Hessians. They foraged and plundered, frightening the inhabitants. The British believed there was plenty of time, and that the Continental Capital was but a day's skirmish away.

Hackensack, Heritage to Horizons

The seal of Hackensack is the bust of the Great Chief of the Lenape Nation, Oratam, who lived from 1577 to 1667 and who negotiated trading with the early Dutch traders.

# DECEMBER 25, 1776 – TOWNSHIP OF HOPEWELL NJ

In December 1776, the Hopewell area, along with most of New Jersey, was under British occupation. This occupation was ended by the famous offensive launched by George Washington which began with the crossing of the Delaware on December 25, 1776, and culminated with the victories at Trenton the next day and at Princeton on January 3, 1777. These events are often called the "ten crucial days of the Revolution." The Continental Army's stream bed crossing of Jacobs Creek on Bear Tavern Road was a prominent event of the march to Trenton on December 26. The view down at the crossing site today from the open, historic truss bridge, still conveys a feeling for the rugged patch of landscape over which tons of artillery, equipment, and supplies were moved with great labor over dangerous frozen ground and a flooding stream on that bitter winter morning.

Thomas Paine publishes "*The Crisis*". Washington has it read to the troops for inspiration prior to the Battle of Trenton.

# DECEMBER 26, 1776 TOWNSHIP OF EWING NJ

The populace of Ewing (Trenton) Township was sympathetic to the American cause during the Revolution, and many served in the war. General George Washington, after ferrying the American army across the Delaware River December 26, 1776, marched his troops down Bear Tavern Road to attack the Hessian mercenary forces stationed in Trenton.

In 1708, Andrew Lockart deeded land on Scotch Road for the establishment of a Presbyterian Church to fulfill the religious needs of the early settlers. The adjacent cemetery contains the graves of many Revolutionary soldiers.

The seal contains an illustration of a Revolutionary soldier and a portrait of Charles Ewing. Ewing Township was named in honor of Charles Ewing, who was Chief Justice of the New Jersey State Supreme Court from 1824-1832.

# DECEMBER 26, 1776 - CITY OF TRENTON NJ

After crossing the Delaware River at night, Washington surprises the Hessians and captures over 900 soldiers without a loss. This single bold stroke by Washington altered the complexion of the war and gave hope to the Revolution after a series of losses.

Among the Hessian soldiers captured were some that had no love for the English. They detested their prince for having sold them into the service of a foreign government and refused to avail themselves of an exchange of prisoners. They then enlisted in the American army and became citizens of the new country.

On July 13, 1793, Council adopted a city seal: "The Divice of which is a Sheaf of Wheat proper, the inscription around the Seal, 'City of Trenton' with the motto E Parvis Grandes (once Small, now Great)." In later years the seal was modified by the placing in of the date "1792" and the elimination of the motto. Three wheat sheaves displaced the one sheaf, and there was added a nag's head, as in the great seal of New Jersey.

# 1777

January 3 – Township of Princeton NJ

January 3 - Mercer County NJ

January 6 – Hillsborough Township NJ

January 6 – Township of Morristown NJ

January 7 – Township of Parsippany
    Troy Hills NJ

January 21 – Township of Franklin NJ

April 20 – Town of Fishkill NY

April 20 – Town of Westport CT

April 26 – Town of Kent NY

April 26 – City of Danbury CT

April 27 – Town of Ridgefield CT

May 10 – Town of Kittery ME

May 21 – Village of Sag Harbor NY

June 14 – Congress authorizes US Flag

June 14 – Borough of Bound Brook NJ

June 14 – Township of Bridgewater NJ

June 14 – Township of Green Brook NJ

July – City of Beacon NY

July 21 – Town of Auburn NH

July 27 – Town of Fort Edward NY

Aug 3 – 20 – City of Rome NY

August 6 – Herkimer County NY

August – Town of Charlestown MD

August 14-16 – Town of Hoosick NY

August 14-16 – Town of Bennington VT

August 16 – Town of New Boston NH

September 11 – Chadds Ford Twnshp PA

September 13 – City of Wilmington DE

September 17 – City of Allentown PA

September 19 – Saratoga County NY

September 20 – Paoli Battlefield PA

September 29 – Skippack Township PA

October 7 – Town of Stillwater NY

October 16 – City of Kingston NY

October 17 – Town of Saratoga NY

October – Borough of Trappe PA

November 15 – County of York PA

November 15 – City of York PA

December 5 – Whitemarsh Township PA

December 13 – Borough of Bridgeport PA

December 19 – Upper Merion Township

# JANUARY 3, 1777 - TOWNSHIP OF PRINCETON NJ

The Battle of Princeton in January of 1777 was recognized as a turning point in the Revolutionary War and made Princeton famous. From June to November 1783 the Second Continental Congress met in Princeton and brought America's new leaders to town. The new State Legislature also met at Princeton.

At the Battle of Princeton, General Hugh Mercer was wounded and cared for under the "Mercer Oak." Although Mercer died nine days later, the Americans won the battle against 1200 British soldiers and along with winning the Battle of Trenton, reversed the string of losses suffered in the previous several months. Continental Marines contributed to the American victory at Princeton.

The seal contains an illustration of the Mercer Oak and is a proud reminder of Princeton's role in the Revolutionary War.

# JANUARY 3, 1777 - MERCER COUNTY NJ

The famous Mercer Oak once stood in the middle of the battlefield, not far from the spot where General Hugh Mercer fell during the Battle of Princeton. The Clarke House, built by Thomas Clarke in 1772, witnessed the fierce fighting and served as sanctuary for General Mercer, who died there nine days later. The house contains period furniture and Revolutionary War exhibits.

General Hugh Mercer gave his name to the oak, to our county and to numerous streets and parks throughout the state of New Jersey. The Mercer Oak came to be more than a symbol of the Revolutionary War. In addition to becoming Princeton Township's logo, it is found in the seals of Mercer County, Mercer Engine No. 3 and the New Jersey State Park Service.

# JANUARY 5, 1777 – HILLSBOROUGH TOWNSHIP NJ

Hillsborough Township quickly took its place in history as the path General Washington and his troops traveled from the Battle of Princeton to winter quarters in Morristown. While the British were encamped in the valley below awaiting an opportunity to attack, it is said that Washington drilled his troops on the Sourland Mountain around a spring near the top using different formations and corn stalks for guns. As the sun caught the stalks, the British thought Washington had received reinforcements and fresh supplies and the British troops, thinking that they were outnumbered, slipped off to New Brunswick leaving Washington to continue to Morristown.

The seal illustrates a Revolutionary era rifle, the scales of justice and an arrow among other symbols important to Hillsborough.

On May 31, 1771, Hillsborough was granted a Charter as a Township.

# THE TOWN OF MORRISTOWN™

## JANUARY 6, 1777 - TOWN OF MORRISTOWN NJ

After the victories at Trenton and Princeton, the Continental Army under General George Washington arrived in Morristown on January 6, 1777. The site was relatively secure lying behind the Watchung Mountains and the Great Swamp, and Washington chose it for the army's winter camp.

The Arnold Tavern on the western edge of the town green became Washington's Headquarters. Rodney's Delaware Light Infantry was quartered on Jacob Ford's property across town. In between, some 2000 officers and soldiers rented quarters in private homes, barns, churches, and other structures throughout Morristown and in towns from Princeton to the Hudson Highlands.

George Washington really did sleep here, for Morristown served as his headquarters for two different winter encampments during the Revolutionary War.

# JANUARY 7, 1777 – TOWNSHIP OF PARSIPPANY - TROY HILLS NJ

By the time Washington and his army were encamped in Morristown, the mills had been turned into munitions factories operating at full blast and continuing all during the Revolution to manufacture shot and shell for the Continental Army.

The first quadrant illustrates a Lenni Lenape village, the first people of this area. The second quadrant is a plow signifying the importance of agriculture.

The third quadrant is a detailed drawing of an iron forge. There were over 70 such mills prior to the Revolution but Britain prohibited the manufacture of many commodities. The ore was shipped to Britain for manufacture and returned to the colonies for profit with appropriate taxes.

In the fourth quadrant of the seal, in addition to the classic symbols of the Revolution, Washington's tri-cornered hat, crossed sword and rifle - - appears a pyramid of cannon balls, which represent the link between the iron industry and the significant part played by this area in the war of the Colonies for their freedom.

- source: 1985 description of the seal from the Office of the Mayor

# JANUARY 21, 1777 - TOWNSHIP OF FRANKLIN NJ

On January 21, 1777, there was a skirmish at the mill between a British foraging party of about 600 troops and a party of Continental soldiers and 300 militia commanded by American General Philemon Dickinson. The British were sent out of New Brunswick by General Cornwallis, seeking the large quantity of flour they believed was stored there. With the bridge at Weston guarded by the British, the American force had to wade across the waist deep, ice filled river. Nevertheless, they so surprised the foraging party the British retreated without ever firing a single one of their three field pieces. In their haste, the British left behind 43 wagons, 164 horses, 118 cattle, 70 sheep and 12 soldiers who became prisoners. In the skirmish, 5 Americans were lost but the British lost about 30 men.

The seal contains an iconic Minute Man with a document and 13 stars.

Seal Adopted 7-10-1990

# APRIL 20, 1777 - TOWN OF FISHKILL NY

The Town of Fishkill seal, showing a Continental Army officer, stalks of wheat, and a scroll representing the first New York State Constitution, printed in Fishkill on April 20, 1777, by Samuel Louden, was sketched by Dr. Herbert Berlin.

The soldier represents the troops stationed in Fishkill 1776-1783. The wheat relates to food and supplies stored at the Fishkill Supply Depot during the Revolution.

Fishkill was incorporated in 1788.

The name Fishkill is derived from two Dutch words: Vis (fish) and Kill (creek or stream). 
- Information provided by Willa Skinner, Historian, Town of Fishkill

# APRIL 25, 1777 - TOWN OF WESTPORT CT

During the Revolutionary War, a battle broke out during the British raid on Danbury. Some 1,850 British soldiers landed on Compo Beach on April 25, 1777, and marched up Compo Road, burning homesteads and barns as they went. After a battle at Ridgefield, the British returned through the village of Saugatuck and fought the local militia in a battle at Compo Hill. The Minute Man statue commemorates this event. The bodies of the colonists killed in this fight are interred at Compo Beach cemetery.

After the Revolutionary War, the Village of Saugatuck began to grow as a shipping center. In the 1830s, 130 villagers made an application to the Connecticut General Assembly to incorporate Westport as a town. The charter was granted May 28, 1835.

The seal was drawn by John Warner Barber. This is a view looking west toward Norwalk. On the far side of the bridge is Riverside Avenue and the right foreground is the site of the old library.

The Town of Westport Seal is used with permission of the Town of Westport.

## APRIL 26, 1777 – TOWN OF KENT NY

It was April of 1777 when the word was out that the British were attacking the Continental supplies at Danbury, just over the line in Connecticut. Col Henry Ludington needed to muster his militia, but it was already dark and the countryside was filled with British soldiers, sympathizers and opportunistic highwaymen. His 16 year old daughter volunteered to go – she knew the roads and the backroads to the homes of every member of the militia. She took her favorite horse named Star and rode over 40 miles at night in the rainstorm. The 400 man militia met the British at Ridgefield the next day.

Sybil was recognized by General George Washington for her efforts and continued to aid her country in a role many women played – that of a messenger.

The Town of Kent seal displays the statue of Sybil Ludington astride Star on her mission. She is known as the female "Paul Revere" of NY although her ride was much longer and more treacherous. Also displayed are heraldic shields.

# APRIL 26, 1777 – CITY OF DANBURY CT

There are 2 references on the seal to the British burning of Danbury when it was burned and looted in April, 1777, by the British under Major General William Tryon because Danbury was an important military depot for the American Revolutionary armies. Nineteen houses and twenty-two storehouses of supplies were destroyed including 1,690 valuable tents.

In the lower left of the Seal is the Wooster Monument, which can be seen entering the Wooster Cemetery's Main entrance on Ellsworth Rd.  It was erected in 1854 to honor General David Wooster who was wounded and died in Ridgefield defending against the British.  The central motto, on a diagonal band which divides the seal, is "Restituimus" or "We have Restored." Underscoring this point, atop the shield, is a phoenix rising from a fiery crown. The bird has in its beak a second motto, "Perege Modo", translated from the Latin as "Ever Onward" or "Let Us Go Forward." The outer circle has the words "Seal of the City of Danbury, incorporated 1889".

Henry Hoyt helped design the seal in 1889, when Danbury officially became a city.

# APRIL 27, 1777 - TOWN OF RIDGEFIELD CT

Ridgefield is the site of the Revolutionary War 1777 "Battle of Ridgefield." American Generals Wooster and Arnold attempted to hold off the British in the only land battle on Connecticut soil during the Revolution. The British had over 1,500 men to the American force of 600 men. There are still monuments and markers to the events or incidents that transpired in that 1777 battle. They remind us that Ridgefield has a heritage that must be preserved. The Revolutionary Road historical project is currently being developed. When it is completed, it will aid all of us in helping to uncover the treasures of Ridgefield, its history, and its patriots. Ridgefield is one of Connecticut's finest treasures.

 The town seal is a result of a local contest.

# MAY 10, 1777 – TOWN OF KITTERY ME

During the Revolution, the first vessels of the U.S. Navy were constructed on Badger's Island, including the 1777 *USS Ranger* commanded by John Paul Jones. The *USS Ranger* was launched on May 10, 1777, at the shipyard of John Langdon in Kittery ME.

During the Revolution, Kittery voted men and means, as they were required of her. Portsmouth Harbor was an important station and war-vessels and privateers were built and fitted out here. The harbor was fortified and garrisoned, both on the New Hampshire and Maine side.

The seal is an illustration of a blockhouse at Ft McClary. The fort was named for Major Andrew McClary of New Hampshire who died at the Battle of Bunker Hill.

# MAY 21, 1777 – VILLAGE OF SAG HARBOR NY

The Village has also contributed to the history of the various wars that were fought on American soil and abroad. The Revolutionary War saw the British set up strong garrisons and naval blockades preventing the Port of Sag Harbor from sending supplies to the American Army. Many of the residents had fled to Connecticut and those that remained suffered tremendous losses as they were robbed, plundered and forced to feed and house the soldiers of the Crown.

On May 21, 1777, Colonel Return Jonathan Meigs, under the command of General Parsons, set off to surprise the British troops in Sag Harbor by making a swift attack and destroying the supplies held by them.  12 sloops and brigs were destroyed in just 25 hours without any casualties to his men.  Over 90 prisoners were captured.

- source - Village website

104

On June 14, 1777, in order to establish an official flag for the new nation, the Continental Congress passed the first Flag Act on a motion by John Adams:

"Resolved, That the flag of the United States be made of thirteen stripes,

alternate red and white; that the union be thirteen stars,

white in a blue field, representing a new Constellation."

The country now had a symbol of unity.

According to Betsy Ross a secret Committee of Three including George Washington, Robert Morris and her uncle Col George Ross met with her in late May of 1777 to sew a new flag. Although never verified, it has been accepted as legend. It is as likely that Francis Hopkinton played a role in designing the flag.

* (Although our flag is not a seal, it shows up in many municipal seals designed after this date).

# JUNE 14, 1777 – BOROUGH OF BOUND BROOK NJ

"Thirteen Star Flag. By special act of Congress, the Betsy Ross flag is flown here 24 hours each day. This is to commemorate Washington's Army having encamped in this area June 14, 1777, the day Congress adopted the Flag Resolution. The period of encampment extended from June 14 to July 2, permitting sufficient time for an official flag to have been brought from Philadelphia to be flown at Middlebrook."

On Sunday, April 13, 1777, a four-column force of 4,000 British Crown troops led by Lord Charles Cornwallis attacked a small American garrison of about 500 commanded by General Benjamin Lincoln and located in the town of Bound Brook. The objective: surround the town, capture the garrison and provisions located at this patriot stronghold and gain a foothold in the war against the American Revolutionary army. In the surprise attack, an advance column led by Hessian Jaeger scouts fighting for the British was pinned down by Colonial soldiers who put up a spirited resistance at the Old Stone Arch Bridge located near the Queens' Bridge.

# JUNE 14, 1777 – TOWNSHIP OF BRIDGEWATER NJ

By special order of Congress, a Thirteen Star Flag is flown 24 hours a day at the Washington Camp Ground, part of the former Middlebrook encampment, in Bridgewater. Since 1889, the first hoisting of the flag is commemorated annually each July 4 with a changing of the flag, a reading of the Declaration of Independence, and the delivery of an historical address.

At the Middlebrook encampment the first official flag of the US was unfurled after a law to adopt a national flag was passed by Congress on June 14, 1777.

 The marker here states:

> "1777 Encampment - The Continental Army camped here from May 28 to July 2, 1777. Advance units were on the slopes facing the Raritan Valley."

# JUNE 14, 1777 - TOWNSHIP OF GREEN BROOK NJ

Also contained within the boundaries of this community is Washington Rock State Park, which commemorates the spot where George Washington and Marquis De Lafayette watched the movement of the British soldiers during the Revolutionary War, mainly the months of May and June 1777. Washington Rock State Park was commissioned on March 17, 1913 and is about 34 acres in size.

Green Brook Township was formed out of a part of North Plainfield Township in 1932. Settlement here was about one hundred years prior to the Revolution on the Passaic River and down in the Valley, which was to become known as Washington's Valley.

# JULY 1777 - CITY OF BEACON NY

Mount Beacon is the most visible summit for miles around, providing the defining backdrop for the local communities. Its prominence made the mountain an important factor in the Revolutionary War, when George Washington's troops set signal fires to communicate vital information about British troop movements.

The mountains provided a key vantage point over West Point and the Hudson River, lending it historic roles in the American Revolution. Signal fires on the mountain gave both it and the nearby city their name. In 1901 the local chapter of the Daughters of the American Revolution erected a monument at the site of the original signal fire near the summit of North Beacon.

In 1913 this new city was christened BEACON in honor of the famous fires which had burned atop the Fishkill Mountain.

# JULY 21, 1777 – TOWN OF AUBURN NH

No battles took place in New Hampshire, but the militia did participate at the Battles of Bunker Hill and the Battle of Bennington. Several Militias were called up in July of 1777 in response to British General Burgoyne's Army attack on Ft Ticonderoga in NY on his way to Saratoga. The NH militia units along with those from Massachusetts and Vermont served under NH General Stark and were victorious at the Battle of Bennington.

254 men served from 1775 to 1782 from Chester. Auburn was once a part of Chester and was incorporated in 1845.

The seal has an illustration of a typical New Hamshire militia man with brown linen breeches. Also illustrated is the rugged geography and terrain common in New Hampshire and Lake Massabesic.

# JULY 27, 1777 - TOWN OF FORT EDWARD NY

Sir William Johnson changed the name of the existing fort from Fort Lyman to Fort Edward on September 21, 1755. It was named in honor of Edward, the Duke of York and Albany, grandson of George II and brother of George III. The town was formally established in 1818.

The seal illustrates the original Fort Edward and references Jane McCrea who was killed and scalped by Indians loyal to the British during the American Revolution. Her death on July 27, 1777, and subsequent failure of the British to punish the guilty parties out of fear of losing their alliance enraged the countryside that took up arms and were partly responsible for defeating Gen Burgoyne and the British at Saratoga in October of that year.

# AUGUST 3-22, 1777 - CITY OF ROME (FORT STANWIX) NY

As part of the British war plan of 1777, Lieutenant Colonel Barry St. Leger led his army eastward across the Mohawk Valley toward Albany. He believed that Fort Stanwix would be lightly defended. His initial demand for surrender in early August was rebuffed by the defenders.

On Aug 3rd, a flag was made from the cloak of Capt Abraham Swartout of Dutchess County NY. It is reported to be the first garrison flag displayed after passage of the flag resolution by Congress on June 14, 1777.

On August 6, 1777, during the Battle of Oriskany Brig Gen Marinus Willett led a sortie from the fort which plundered the nearby Indian and Sir John Johnson's Tories camp. His force suffered no casualties. When the Tories and their Indian allies returned from the Battle of Oriskany, they found their plundered camp and the Indians all left. Fearing more patriot reinforcements, St. Ledger returned to Canada on August 22nd and Burgoyne was denied his reinforcements.

# AUGUST 6, 1777 – HERKIMER COUNTY NY

Battle of Oriskany - A 1,200-man detachment from St. Leger's army, mostly Mohawks and Loyalists, was lying in wait for the 800 man American relief column for the siege of Ft Stanwix. The initial volley cut down most of the American leadership, including Gen Nicholas Herkimer who sustained a serious leg wound. He had his men prop him up against a tree and continued to direct the battle. Despite his efforts, the Americans were eventually forced from the field. Both sides suffered heavy losses at Oriskany. The battle has been described as the bloodiest battle of the American Revolution. 200 Americans were killed and another 200 taken prisoner. Virtually all of the combatants were American, and many were familiar with individuals on the other side. Herkimer died shortly thereafter.

The British army in the Mohawk Valley failed to keep its rendezvous with Burgoyne at Albany, a failure that contributed heavily to the events around Saratoga in the following weeks.

The seal illustrates Nicholas Herkimer directing the battle despite his wounds.

113

## AUGUST 1777 – TOWN OF CHARLESTOWN MD

During the Revolutionary War, Charlestown was a major supply depot for the Continental Army.

Two incidents in Charlestown are recorded from the Revolutionary War. The first involved a blockading, British warship in the Charlestown Harbor that was captured and burned. The ship's officers and men were marched through the streets of the Town. In August, 1777, the town was bombarded as a diversionary tactic while General Sir William Howe's troops sailed 264 ships up the Elk River to effect a landing. General Howe landed his approximately 15,000 troops at the Head of Elk, subsequently marching them north and culminating in the Battle of Brandywine.

The original seal of Charlestown was ordered on June 26, 1796, "with the devise of a ship and **CHARLESTOWN CECIL COUNTY MARYLAND** round the edge in capital letters …" and bespeaks a time when Charlestown was a major port.

# AUGUST 14-16, 1777 - TOWN OF HOOSICK NY

The most historical event to occur in the Town was the Revolutionary War Battle of Bennington which was fought on and about a hilltop in Walloomsac, Town of Hoosick, NY.

Here, General John Stark, Colonel Seth Warner and the Green Mountain Boys defeated some of Europe's best regular soldiers. The British and Hessians had over 200 casualties vs. 40 for the Americans. The Americans took over 700 prisoners.

The result of this battle was disastrous to General Burgoyne's campaign, and contributed more than any other event to his final surrender at Saratoga.

The seal honors the Revolutionary War, the arts, agriculture and industry in the Town. It was adopted in 2002 for the Town's 175th anniversary celebration.

115

## AUGUST 14-16, 1777 - TOWN OF BENNINGTON  VT

In the late summer of 1777, the Continental Army beat a hasty retreat toward Bennington. British and Hessians pursued, but were badly in need of supplies.

The Americans defeated them before they could reach the supply depot at Bennington.  The British were forced to proceed to Saratoga without the supplies, where they met a stunning defeat that turned the tide of the Revolutionary War.

The seal depicts the Bennington Battle Monument which commemorates the Battle of Bennington that occurred on August 14-16, 1777, where the Americans under Gen John Stark defeated the British and the Hessians, just prior to the Battle of Saratoga. The monument soars more than 300 feet above the lovely streets of Old Bennington, the site of a critical military supply depot.

August 16th is celebrated annually in Vermont as Bennington Battle Day.

# AUGUST 16, 1777 – TOWN OF NEW BOSTON NH

*"The famous Molly Stark cannon, captured from the British at the battle of Bennington (VT) by New Hampshire troops under the command of General John Stark on August 16, 1777, has for many generations been the proud possession of the citizens of New Boston. She is two hundred and twenty years old, having been cast in Paris, France, in 1743. Old Molly, as we affectionately call her, has had a most glorious history, serving under the French flag once, the British twice and the American twice."*

- **excerpt from "The New Boston Artillery Company and Molly Stark" Clement A. Lyon 1963**

General John Stark popularized the phrase, "Live Free or Die."

# SEPTEMBER 11, 1777 - CHADDS FORD TOWNSHIP PA

Battle of Brandywine

- With an estimated 29,000 troops actively engaged, it was the largest land battle in the Revolutionary War.
- It was one of the few encounters where the two commanders-in chief (General George Washington and General Sir William Howe) were both in command on the battlefield.
- Despite their loss of the field, it inspired the Continental soldiers to continue the fight.
- It is thought to have been the first battle in which the rapid-firing breech-loading Patrick Ferguson rifle was used by the British.
- It is believed to have been the first battle in which the Betsy Ross flag was flown.

Washington was forced to retreat and eventually Howe occupied Philadelphia. The Continental Congress left Philadelphia also. Among the wounded on this day was the Marquis de Lafayette and a young John Marshall who would one day become Chief Justice of the US Supreme Court.

# SEPTEMBER 13, 1777 - CITY OF WILMINGTON DE

From the granting of the charter in 1739 until the Revolution, the town developed steadily. During the Revolution, its milling industries, geographic location, key leaders and resources made Wilmington particularly strategic.

The summer of 1777 found Wilmington in the center of the struggle for American independence. George Washington established Revolutionary army headquarters in Wilmington, as did General Anthony Wayne. British troops landed in Maryland and marched across Delaware toward Philadelphia. American troops met the British at Cooch's Bridge on Sept. 3, 1777, but were forced to retreat into Pennsylvania. The British took Wilmington on the 13th, following the Battle of Brandywine, and the town became a British camp until the end of October 1777.

Wilmington's city seal was adopted in 1832, when it received a city charter from the state. It shows a mill, representing the early flour milling industry; sailing ships to represent the city's shipping industry; and a plow, to symbolize agriculture.

# SEPTEMBER 17, 1777 - CITY OF ALLENTOWN PA

Forced to evacuate Philadelphia, the Continental Congress ordered that all bells and chimes be removed so that their metal could not be melted down and cast into bullets by the enemy. Most important of all these pieces was the Liberty Bell, which was then hanging in the Old State House. According to Congress, the Liberty Bell was to be secretly conveyed to Allentown and secured until Philadelphia could be retaken. Hidden under straw and potato sacks in a wagon train of a Pennsylvania Dutch farmer who had come to the city to sell produce, the bell began its journey to safety on September 17. The British marched into Philadelphia on the 26th.

The bells were hidden under the floor of the Zion High German Reformed Church (now United Church of Christ) in center city Allentown. In June of 1778, the British had broken camp in Philadelphia and were headed north. The bells were returned after the British evacuated Philadelphia. Farmers John Jacob Mickley and Frederick Loeser both have commemorative tablets in Pennsylvania which honor the parts they played in the saving of the Liberty Bell.

# SEPTEMBER 19, 1777 – SARATOGA COUNTY NY

When news that Gen Howe had decided to attack Philadelphia rather than meet Burgoyne, and St Ledger had been turned back at Rome, Washington dispatched Col Daniel Morgan's Rifle Corps with 500 elite sharpshooters to Saratoga. Gen Lincoln cut Burgoyne's supply lines to the north by recapturing Whitehall. Also present in Saratoga was Col John Glover from Marblehead MA.

On September 19th the riflemen were particularly effective at picking off the artillerymen so that the British cannons were not effective. The battle ended in a draw.

The seal is an illustration of the battlefield with the new American flag and a regiment of grenadiers supported by cannon.

## SEPTEMBER 20-21, 1777 – PAOLI PA

The Battle of Paoli has also been referred to as the "Paoli Massacre." It was a small, vicious battle that occurred during the Revolution at midnight on September 20-21, 1777. Reports of the day indicate the British gave no quarter and took very few prisoners, bayoneting the Americans, thus the battle cry, "Remember Paoli!"

Efforts to commemorate the battle and preserve the grave of those who died have a long history. In 1817 on the 40th anniversary of the attack, a monument was placed on the grave and a stone wall was constructed to protect it. This monument is the second oldest Revolutionary War battle monument (the Lexington Monument was dedicated on July 4, 1799). Adjacent land, eventually was acquired to serve as a drill field and parade ground for Chester and Delaware County militia in the 19th century.

The logo belongs to the Paoli Battlefield Preservation Fund and their website is www.ushistory.org/paoli/about/index.htm. Encampments and parades commemorating the battle were held regularly for many years in proximity to the Paoli Tavern, a well-known landmark in 1777.

# SEPTEMBER 29, 1777 – SKIPPACK TOWNSHIP PA

Quite a few structures, including the Indenhofen house and farm, were already here in Skippack when George Washington and his Continental Army positioned themselves in the region before and after the important Battle of Germantown. George Washington camped near the Indenhofen house on September 29, 1777 with about 10,000 militia and regulars before he went on down the Skippack Road to fight the Battle of Germantown.

Researched and written by Bradley S. DeForest, Member of Skippack Historical Society

After the Battle at Chadds Ford, the Americans were forced to evacuate Philadelphia. The British moved in and occupied the city. George Washington looked for a way to drive the British out and the resulting plan was the Battle of Germantown fought on October 4. Through the fog and smoke of the nearly 3 hour battle, the Americans retreated, but proved they could stand up to the British Army.

*"The Township of Skippack Seal is used with permission of the Township of Skippack"*

# OCTOBER 7, 1777 - TOWN OF STILLWATER NY

The town furnished the field for the Battles of Bemis Heights - or Saratoga and half of the 13th Albany Militia Regiment that helped defeat the British on October 7, 1777, now officially one of the 15 most decisive battles of the world.

Tim Murphy, one of Daniel Morgan's sharpshooters, killed Gen Simon Fraser and Sir Francis Clarke from a distance of 300 yards. The loss of these two officers and the arrival of American General Tenbroek with an additional 3000 troops from New York left the British demoralized and led directly to Burgoyne's eventual defeat.

Nearly 500 British soldiers were killed and another 700 wounded during this battle. This area is now the Saratoga National Historical Park.

The Town itself was formed in 1791, and the Village was incorporated in 1816.

# OCTOBER 16, 1777- CITY OF KINGSTON NY

In 1777 the British forces had reason to see the village of Kingston as a hotbed of perfidy and sedulous disloyalty to King George the Third and His Majesty's Parliament. The farmers near Kingston had provided Washington's troops with wheat and other food supplies. In September of 1777, John Jay and other leading patriots met in a stone house in Kingston to declare the province a sovereign state and establish the first New York State Senate. In a nearby building, the first State Assembly met. Kingston became New York State's first capital.

In October, General William Clinton brought British forces up the Hudson on the way to meet Burgoyne coming down from Canada. It was an opportunity to punish Kingston. Landing at nearby Kingston Point, British Major General Vaughn's forces marched on the village and put the torch to every barn (103) and house (116) in the village but one. The residents fled to Hurley, a smaller village several miles away.

The Senate House on the seal represents Kingston's contribution, as first Capitol, to the history of New York State.

Site of Burgoyne's Surrender • Revolutionary War Turning Point •

TOWN OF SARATOGA • ESTABLISHED MARCH 7, 1788

October 17, 1777

# OCTOBER 17, 1777 – TOWN OF SARATOGA NY

After the 2nd Battle of Saratoga, Burgoyne was left with 6000 soldiers and was now surrounded by over 20,000 Americans. Gen Stark held the position now called Stark's Knob and prevented Burgoyne's Army from escaping to the North back to Canada.

General Clinton was stalled near Kingston and would not be bringing relief supplies as planned so on 17 October, Burgoyne surrendered his army near Saratoga. The capitulation was a turning point of the war for it induced the French to sign a military alliance with the infant American Republic in February 1778.

Although Benedict Arnold and Daniel Morgan were primarily responsible for the victory, Gen Gates took the credit for himself.

The seal commemorates the Surrender of Burgoyne after the British were defeated. The scene is a black and white version from the famous painting by John Trumbull. Col Daniel Morgan is seen dressed in white buckskin. Some reports indicate we played Yankee Doodle Dandy at the surrender.

# OCTOBER 1777 - BOROUGH OF TRAPPE PA

The Borough of Trappe uses the design of their flag as other municipalities use their seal, i.e. on their website and stationery, etc.

The symbols are arranged in a shield divided into four parts.

Upper right: An outline drawing of old Augustus Lutheran, the oldest unaltered church in the United States, symbolizes the religious faith of the people of Trappe. Lower right: The founding representative government with liberty and justice for all consumed a great deal of time and energy of the people of Trappe during the American Revolution and the years thereafter. The sword reminds us that through September and October 1777 the Continental Armies occupied Trappe. The pen rests on top of the sword to remind us that the pen is mightier than the sword. Lower left: The early colonial settlement in 1717 is symbolized by the log cabin. The first was built by Jacob Schrack. Upper left: Farming and industry are portrayed by the rake, the fork and the cog wheels. 1717 and 1896 are the dates of founding and the incorporation of the borough.

# NOVEMBER 15, 1777 - COUNTY OF YORK PA

Adopted by Congress on November 15, 1777, the Articles became operative on March 1, 1781 when the last of the 13 states signed on to the document. The country that declared independence on July 4, 1776, now had an official government.

The central illustration is the Articles of Confederation and a Quill over an outline of the County.

The Continental Congress was meeting in York since the British had defeated Washington at Chadds Ford and now occupied Philadelphia. The City of York claims to be the nation's first capital – until June 27, 1778 when the British left Philadelphia.

# NOVEMBER 15, 1777 – CITY OF YORK PA

The City of York, Pennsylvania - named for York, England - was part of the building of our nation, a little-known part of history that many tend to forget, or just don't know. As Yorkers know, their City was the birthplace of the Articles of Confederation and it was here that the words "The United States of America" were first spoken.

In September of 1777 the Continental Congress, under threat of the advancing British, moved the location of the colonies' central government from Philadelphia to Lancaster. Since the State of Pennsylvania's Government was also located in Lancaster, officials decided that a move across the Susquehanna would separate the two sufficiently and the Continental Congress set up shop in the Town of York.

It was in York that the Congress adopted the Articles of Confederation, proclaimed the first National Day of Thanksgiving, and signed the French Treaty of Alliance. All of these events occurred in the nine months York remained Capital of the United States - until June 27, 1778.

## DECEMBER 5, 1777 - WHITEMARSH TOWNSHIP PA

During the Revolution, Whitemarsh hosted several important events relating to the war. During the fall of 1777, General Washington and 11,000 troops were stationed in the township, guarding the Wissahickon Valley from British redcoats, who then held Philadelphia. Washington's encampment extended from Militia Hill on the west, over Fort and Camp Hills, to Edge Hill on the east.

The Battle of Whitemarsh took place during December 5, 6, and 7, 1777. It was a series of skirmishes between the Revolutionaries and General Howe's troops in the Flourtown area. They ended when a British attempt to capture Fort Hill was thwarted because their cannons could not traverse the terrain between Flourtown and the Hill. The British then moved into winter quarters in the City of Philadelphia. Shortly after that Washington and his troops decamped for Valley Forge.

The seal has a cannon and pyramid of cannon balls symbolizing this history.

130

Bridgeport,
Bridge to Valley Forge

# DECEMBER 13, 1777 - BRIDGEPORT PA

The movement to Valley Forge was begun on December 1. The army went by way of " Sweeds" Ford (Norristown), where, as the quaint diary of Albigence Waldo says:

"A Bridge of Waggons made across the Schuylkill last night consisted of 36 waggons, with a bridge of Rails between each. Sun Set—We are order'd to march over the River. The Army were 'till Sun Rise crossing the River—some at the Waggon Bridge, & some at the Raft Bridge below. Cold and Uncomfortable."

This illustration has George Washington and his army superimposed over the actual seal of Bridgeport, underscoring the history and significance of the Borough of Bridgeport. This is the cover of the book that was published by the Borough in 1976.

# DECEMBER 19, 1777 - UPPER MERION TOWNSHIP PA

**VALLEY FORGE -** On the sixth of December, 1777, Washington, with his army, left Whitemarsh, and on the afternoon of the 13th crossed at Swedes' Ford and proceeded towards the Gulf and the vicinity of King of Prussia, where they remained until the 19th. They arrived at Valley Forge, where they were to remain until the following 18th day of June, exactly six months.

It was here that the Army suffered one of its most trying times and was reborn with the help of Baron Von Steuben as an army capable of meeting the British as equals.

"When the Continental Army wintered here, every acre was heavily used – for entrenchments, stock pens, an artillery park, and parade grounds. Fields turned to mud. Within decades after the war, the scene had returned to woodlots and farmland. The tour route circles the encampment, now marked by earthworks and monuments."

Highway Marker – Valley Forge

# 1778

1778 - Town Of Durham CT

Winter 1778 – E Norriton Township PA

1778 - Oneida Indian Nation

April 30 - Borough of Ringwood NJ

April 30 - Town of Warwick NY

May 1 - Borough of Hatboro PA

May 28 – Town of Clarksville IN

May 28 – City of Louisville KY

June 28 - Borough of Englishtown NJ

June 28 - Township of Manalapan NJ

June 28 - Freehold Township NJ

July 3 – City of Sunbury PA

July – Village of Port Jefferson NY

August 29 - Town of Tiverton RI

August 29 - City of Newport RI

September 19 - Town of Patterson NY

September 28 - Township of River Vale NJ

September 30 - Village of Hastings on Hudson NY

October 16 - Township of Little Egg Harbor NJ

October 17 - Town of Pawling NY

November – Village of Fishkill NY

# WINTER OF 1777 / 1778 - TOWN OF DURHAM CT

In 1777, two oxen presented by Durhamites were driven 500 miles to Valley Forge to feed officers of Washington's Army.

The town seal was adopted on September 16, 1975.

1776 - 1781 Revolutionary War – 103 men served.

*Seal of the Town of Durham. The ox was chosen because it symbolizes strength and tenacity, qualities needed for survival in the new country. It also represents Durham's agricultural history. Finally, oxen figured prominently in Durham's Revolutionary War experience. In the winter of 1777-78 the town of Durham sent a pair of oxen to Valley Forge, Pennsylvania where General George Washington was headquartered with his troops, half-starved and enduring bitter weather. The oxen "furnished a dinner for all of the officers of the American Armies . . . and all their servants."*

# WINTER 1778 – EAST NORRITON TOWNSHIP PA

The current township seal was created by local artist John Yaworski for the celebration in 1976 marking the bicentennial of the United States.

The seal depicts George Washington and Bartle Bartleson's Tavern which was located on today's Germantown Pike. There Gen Washington visited wounded troops in the township during the Revolutionary War.

Martha Washington joined her husband at Valley Forge from February through June of 1778 and frequently tended to the sick and wounded soldiers.

# 1778 – ONEIDA INDIAN NATION

Polly Cooper was an Oneida woman who according to Oneida oral tradition, walked several hundred miles from her home in Central New York to Valley Forge in the cruel winter of 1777-78 to help feed Gen George Washington's starving troops. Polly Cooper, along with several dozen warrior Oneidas, carried barrels of corn to feed the troops. The corn they brought was white corn and different from the yellow version that is prepared simply. By contrast, the white corn requires extended preparation before it can be eaten. The soldiers, however, were desperate for food when Polly Cooper and her fellow Oneidas arrived, and they tried to eat the corn uncooked. The Oneidas stopped the soldiers, knowing that if they ate the raw corn it would swell in their stomachs and kill them. Congress offered to compensate Polly Cooper but she refused and Martha Washington gave her a shawl still in possession of descendents.

Each clan, wolf, turtle and bear is displayed in the tree of life. The eagle sitting on top of the tree is a protector. The tree of peace is said to be a great white pine tree. The wampum belt symbolizes the six nations in the Haudenosaunee Confederacy.

*The Oneida Nation Seal is used with permission from the Oneida Indian Nation.*

# APRIL 30, 1778 – BOROUGH OF RINGWOOD NJ

The Borough of Ringwood was incorporated on February 23, 1918. Early in the 18th Century, iron was discovered in the area, and the Ogden family built a blast furnace there in 1742. By 1765, Peter Hasenclever used Ringwood as the center of his ironmaking operations. Iron mining was prominent in the area from the 1700s until the Great Depression.

During the American Revolutionary War, Robert Erskine managed ironmaking operations from Ringwood, and became George Washington's first geographer and Surveyor-General, producing maps for the Continental Army. Washington visited the Manor House several times. Ringwood iron was used in the famous Hudson River Chain and for tools and hardware for the army.

The seal is an illustration of the forge at colonial Ringwood. The chain links symbolize the Chain across the Hudson River.

# APRIL 30, 1778 – TOWN OF WARWICK NY

The key element of the West Point/Constitution Island fortifications was the "Great Chain" affixed across the river as of 30 April 1778. Ships which successfully negotiated the bend in the river would still confront the chain barrier, which was expected to bring them to a dead stop, thus facilitating engagement by batteries on the river banks.

The West Point chain was forged at Sterling Ironworks in Warwick, NY. It was approximately 500 yards in length, composed of two foot long, 2.25" thick iron links, each of which weighed 114 pounds. The entire chain weighed in at 65 tons and required 40 men four days to install. The chain floated on rafts assembled from 4 16' sharpened logs, anchored between Constitution Island and West Point.

The chain links across the center of the seal symbolize the Hudson River Chain. Patrick F. Egan designed the Seal of the Town of Warwick and it was officially adopted by the Town Board of the Town of Warwick on October 18, 1971.

# MAY 1, 1778 – BOROUGH OF HATBORO PA

Hatboro played a role in the Revolutionary War. In the summer of 1777, on the way to his Moland House headquarters, George Washington and his officers stopped for dinner at the Crooked Billet Tavern. He bought his grain from the old grist mill that is now the Old Mill Inn. It is said that hats were made in Hatboro for the Revolutionary War soldiers.

Hatboro was also the scene of a Revolutionary War skirmish, known as the Battle of Crooked Billet. The clash occurred on May 1, 1778, during the British occupation of Philadelphia. The militia, commanded by General John Lacey and assigned to cut off British supplies, was encamped here. Surprised by British troops, they were defeated and driven off with heavy losses. Today there is a monument to this battle outside the Crooked Billet Elementary School.

# MAY 1778 – TOWN OF CLARKSVILLE IN

The Town of Clarksville, which bills itself as the "Oldest American Town in the Northwest Territory", was chartered in 1783 by the Virginia legislature. The original town was composed of 1,000 acres set aside from the grant of 150,000 acres the legislature donated to George Rogers Clark and his men.

The Falls of the Ohio, a series of rapids along the 350 million-year-old Devonian fossil beds, created a natural stopping point for settlers and commerce moving west along the Ohio River. The rapids also created a natural defense for Gen George Rogers Clark and the families of the troops he gathered for an assault on the British forces in 1778 and 1779. This area played a major part in the story of Revolutionary War hero George Rogers Clark.

Clark's successful campaign against the British in the Northwest Territory was the basis of a continuous connection to the area that would become Clarksville until his death in 1818.

# MAY 28, 1778 – CITY OF LOUISVILLE KY

Across the Ohio River from the Town of Clarksville, at the Falls of the Ohio is the City of Louisville. George Rogers Clark is considered the founder of the city.

While the rest of the colonies were fighting the British, George Rogers Clark essentially won the Northwest Territory which doubled the size of the country by the time the treaty was signed in 1783.

The city was named for the French King Louis 16th. France officially decided to help finance the war and declared war on Britain in February of 1778.

This seal was designed in 1949 by Austrian typographer Victor Hammer and replaced in 2003 when the city merged with Jefferson County. The seal has 13 stars, the date of the first settlement and the symbol of French royalty, the Fleur de lis.

# JUNE 28, 1778 - BOROUGH OF ENGLISHTOWN NJ

During the Battle of Monmouth, Englishtown was the headquarters for the American Army. The night after the battle General Washington and his officers were invited to the home of Moses Laird to partake of a special "collation" prepared by his wife and daughters. This house is now the Hulse Memorial Home, Main Street, which was built by Moses Laird as a two room tavern before the revolution.

In 1777 one of the Monmouth County's main roads ran from Monmouth Court House, now Freehold, to Englishtown and on into Middlesex County. Because Englishtown was on a main highway, it became a trading center for the surrounding country side.

The seal was drawn by Charles Wykoff most likely in 1976.

# JUNE 28, 1778 - TOWNSHIP OF MANALAPAN NJ

Manalapan was the site of the Battle of Monmouth, a Revolutionary War engagement held on June 28, 1778, involving up to 23,000 British and Continental troops. On the two hundredth anniversary of the Battle the State opened the 1,520 acre Monmouth Battlefield State Park. Eighty percent of the Park is in Manalapan Township. A reenactment of the Battle is held annually on or near June 28.

Baron Von Steuben's training during the winter paid off and 11,000 Americans faced 10,000 British on their own terms and fought to at least a draw. George Washington relieved a retreating General Lee of command and personally rallied the troops.

Wounded in the battle were 16 year old Peter Francisco and 21 year old Marquis de Lafayette who became friends for life while recuperating together.

# JUNE 28, 1778 - FREEHOLD TOWNSHIP NJ

The Battle of Monmouth was fought at its doorsteps on a scorching day in June 1778. The battle lasted all day and several hundred men died of heat stroke.

Every major American military leader of the time participated: George Washington, Marquis de Lafayette, Benedict Arnold, Anthony Wayne, Charles Lee, Alexander Hamilton, Nathanael Greene and Friedrich van Steuben. This is also the battle where the legend of Molly Pitcher originated. While some details are in dispute, the wife of an artillery man took his place when he fell.

This battle ultimately forced the British to change their strategy and look to winning the war in the south.

# JULY 3, 1778 - CITY OF SUNBURY PA

Sunbury became the site of one of the most important frontier forts in Pennsylvania - Fort Augusta. Fort Augusta was a reliable stronghold during the days of the French and Indian War. It also played a major role in the Revolutionary War where it served as the military headquarters for the American Forces in the Upper Susquehanna Valley. On July 3rd, over 700 Loyalists and Iroquois ambushed about 300 American militia in the Wyoming valley. The prisoners were tortured and 227 scalps taken.

That massacre and others sent settlers fleeing to Fort Augusta seeking protection in what came to be known as "the Big Runaway." Colonel Hartley restored order briefly but in July of 1779 Native American raids began again and "the Little Runaway" occurred.

A young woman, Rachael Silverthorn and soldier Robert Covenhoven rode through dangerous territory to warn the settlers to leave.

# JULY 1778 - VILLAGE OF PORT JEFFERSON NY

Drowned Meadow residents played a key role in the Revolutionary War participating in the Culper Spy Ring on Long Island in 1778 to gather critical intelligence for General Washington. Benjamin Tallmadge was a classmate of Nathan Hale and also taught school in Connecticut before the Revolutionary War. His code name was John Bolton. He grew up on Long Island and had childhood friends that he trusted. One was Abraham Woodhull whose code name was Samuel Culper.

Anna Smith Strong, known as "Nancy" Strong used her wash line to signal the Spy Ring so messages from Manhattan to Long Island could be passed to Connecticut. It was the Culper Spy Ring that discovered the treachery of Benedict Arnold. After the war, Washington traveled to the area to thank the residents for their support.

In 1836, Drowned Meadow was renamed Port Jefferson, in honor of President Thomas Jefferson.

# AUGUST 29, 1778 – TOWN OF TIVERTON RI

Battle of Rhode Island - For approximately three years during the Revolution (1776 - 1779) when the British held Aquidneck Island, Tiverton was an asylum for Americans fleeing from British occupation, and the town became a mustering point for Colonial forces who gathered together to drive the British off the island. The lower right quadrant depicts a cannon from the Revolutionary Fort Barton.

During the American Revolution these "Tiverton Highlands" represented an important strategic location for preventing an invasion of the mainland across the narrow Sakonnet River strait by British Forces who occupied Aquidneck Island.

Consequently, the Massachusetts Bay Colony commissioned a defensive fortification, originally called Tiverton Heights Fort.

An extensive system of earthen ramparts was constructed and defended by artillery. At one point the fort was manned by several thousand colonial troops. This was during the staging for an unsuccessful invasion of Aquidneck Island known as the Battle of Rhode Island on August 29, 1778.

# AUGUST 29, 1778 – CITY OF NEWPORT RI

Newport helped lead the way toward the American Revolution and independence. Because the city was such a well-known hot-bed of revolutionary fervor and because of its long history of disdain for royal and parliamentary efforts to control its trade, the British occupied Newport from 1776 to 1779, and over half of the town's population fled. The British remained in Newport despite efforts to drive them out in 1778 by patriot forces in partnership with the French for the first time in the Revolution. Eventually the British did withdraw and the French, under the leadership of Admiral deTiernay and General Rochambeau, began a sojourn in Newport that lasted until 1781 when they left Newport on their historic march to Yorktown to assist in the decisive victory there.   Source: City of Newport

The seal illustrates the seaport at a later period in Newport's history.

*The seal of the City of Newport is the property of the City of Newport.*

PATTERSON, NY

# SEPTEMBER 19, 1778 – TOWN OF PATTERSON NY

During the Revolution the present Town of Patterson and surrounding region was known as Fredericksburg. Between September 19 and November 28, 1778, Washington was headquartered in the house of John Kane, which today is located on Quaker Hill in Pawling. His forces, the second line, commanded by Major General Lord Sterling, numbering 17,000, were encamped in what is now Patterson.

It is little known that Fredericksburg can boast of hosting as varied a group of notable officers as any in the county. Many Generals were on hand for a large celebration of the victory at Saratoga the previous year. Careful study has disclosed none other than Alexander Hamilton also visited the area. A second smaller Revolutionary Army camp was established in town by the Marquis de Lafayette in the winter of 1780. by John J. Bodor in 1976, then the Historian for the Town of Patterson

Matthew Paterson, after whom the town is named, was a native of Scotland who came to this country in 1752. The original name of our town was spelled "Paterson", but was changed to its current spelling in the mid 19th century because of continuing confusion in the mail system with Paterson, New Jersey.

# SEPTEMBER 28, 1778 - TOWNSHIP OF RIVER VALE NJ

On September 28, 1778, the British troops under Major-General Charles Grey used their bayonets to surprise Americans under Colonel Baylor. Grey had previously used bayonets at the Battle of Paoli. His troops went from house to house and killed or injured at least 69 of the dragoons. Eleven were killed outright; four were left and died of their wounds. Colonel Baylor was wounded and captured—he died in 1784 from complications of the wounds incurred in the attack.

In 1967, a mass grave site was discovered in River Vale from that event that occurred in 1778 during the American Revolutionary War known as the Baylor Massacre. The burial site eventually was made into a county park and dedicated on October 15, 1972.

The seal features a musket with a horn of gun powder and an outline of the Township in front of an American flag.

# SEPTEMBER 30, 1778 - VILLAGE OF HASTINGS ON HUDSON NY

During the American Revolution, what is now Hastings lay between the lines of the warring forces and was declared neutral territory. In reality, the area became a no-man's land and was raided repeatedly by both sides.

The Battle of Edgar's Lane was fought on September 30, 1778.

> *Continental Dragoons Under Maj. Henry Lee killed 23 Hessians on a Marauding Expedition. Battle Waged Here to Ravine* – Highway Marker

Henry "Light Horse Harry" Lee would be promoted to Col by the end of the War and chosen by Congress to give the eulogy when George Washington died in 1799.

He is also known as the father of Robert E. Lee.

## OCTOBER 16, 1778 – TOWNSHIP of LITTLE EGG HARBOR NJ

With the British holding Philadelphia and New York, during that awful winter of 1777-78, General Washington at Valley Forge had his source of supplies cut off. Supplies were then brought into Little Egg Harbor, unloaded at Chestnut Neck, taken up the river on flat boats to the Forks, carted across the state to Burlington, and on to Valley Forge. Many cargoes intended for Sir Henry Clinton in New York, because of our privateers, reached General Washington at Valley Forge. Thus, Little Egg Harbor proved a real life line during that darkest period of the War.

Count Pulaski arrives at Chestnut Neck on October 8th. Here he and the British watched each other until October 15th when, through the treachery of a deserter, the British were able to surprise an outpost of fifty of Pulaski's men, bayonet the sentry and almost the entire number of men. It is said that the order for "no quarter" had been given. There were 200 of the British and 50 of Count Pulaski's men. This is known as the "Massacre of Little Egg Harbor." The British then sailed back to New York.

# OCTOBER 17, 1778 – TOWN OF PAWLING NY

George Washington occupied the Kane house (featured on the seal) for two months in 1778. During that time there was a celebration in honor of Gen Gates on the one year anniversary of Burgoyne's surrender at Saratoga with a three day ox roast.

"A section of the Continental Army of the Revolutionary War was stationed on the western slopes of Quaker Hill from September 16, to November 28, 1778. The Great Barbecue Occurred on the hillside across this road.
October 17, 1778. It commemorated the first anniversary of the surrender of the British under Gen. Burgoyne to the Americans at Saratoga, New York. General George Washington Led the parade from his headquarters at the John Kane house. Among the officers present were Major Generals Gates, Greene, McDougall, Baron Steuben, Baron DeKalb, Brigadier Generals Nixon, Parsons, Smallwood, Knox, Hand, Patterson, and Wayne. Sky rockets and cannon were discharged in honor of the celebration."

Tablet erected by the Historical Society of Quaker Hill and Pawling
Contributed by the West Mountain Mission

# OCTOBER 1778 - VILLAGE OF FISHKILL NY

On August 14, 1776 the Provincial Congress meeting at White Plains resolved to quarter troops at Fishkill, establish hospitals and depots for provisions and "convert the place into an armed camp." During 1778, the Village of Fishkill became part of one of the largest Colonial military encampments during the Revolutionary War. General Washington's aide-de-camp, Alexander Hamilton took residence here. In 1778, the Fishkill military complex served as headquarters for the Northern Department of the Continental Army. It remained so through the end of the war.

The Fishkill Supply Depot and Encampment was critical to the success of the Continental Army during the American Revolution and was central to the founding of the United States. Documents show that its importance to General Washington as an essential military facility cannot be overestimated.

The Village of Fishkill was incorporated on May 21, 1899. The seal of a Continental Soldier symbolizes the Fishkill Encampment.

# 1779

January – Town of Washington CT

February 18 – Township of Bedminster NJ

February 25 – City of Vincennes IN

February 26 – Town of Greenwich CT

July 5 – Town of East Haven CT

July 5 – City of West Haven CT

July 11 – City of Norwalk CT

July 11 – Town of Trumbull CT

July 15-16 – Town of Stony Point NY

July 22 – Town of Highland NY

August 13 – Chemung County NY

August 29 – Town of Ashland NY

September 14 – Town of Leicester NY

September 24 – Village of Horseheads NY

October 9 – City of Savannah GA

# JANUARY 1779 - TOWN OF WASHINGTON CT

"As the first town to be incorporated in Connecticut after the Declaration of Independence was signed, Washington bears the name of the Revolutionary War General who passed through the area on three separate occasions, George Washington. " - from town website as published by *Voices Newspaper*, May 2002

The eastern section of what is now Washington was settled by Joseph Hurlbut in 1734 and was known as the Parish of Judea and belonged to Woodbury. The western section was known as the Parish of New Preston and belonged to New Milford. These and others were formed into the Town of Washington in January 1779.

Major Cogswell was not just a soldier and politician, but also the owner of a fabled tavern along the "turnpike." General Washington himself dined at "Squire Cogswell's" tavern in May of 1781.

Thirty Revolutionary soldiers were buried in the original Judea Cemetery.

# FEBRUARY 18, 1779 - TOWNSHIP OF BEDMINSTER NJ

One of the most noted events in Pluckemin was The Grand Alliance Ball on February 18, 1779. General and Mrs. Washington and 400 others attended the celebration of the one year anniversary of the French Alliance. The celebration began with the firing of 13 cannon at 4:00 pm followed by a fireworks display, dinner and dancing. Many toasts were drunk to patriotic sentiments.

The Jacobus Vanderveer House on Rt 206 and the Pluckemin Encampment on Schley Mountain where Colonial militia were trained on artillery equipment are two reminders of the Township of Bedminster's role in the Revolutionary War.

Winter of 1778-1779 – General Henry Knox and his family lived in the Jacobus Vanderveer House. Pluckemin was the site of a massive Revolutionary War artillery encampment. It included an artillery school established by General Knox that was the forerunner of West Point.

157

# FEBRUARY 25, 1779 - CITY OF VINCENNES IN

Founded in 1732, it was George Rogers Clark and his small army who took the largest land conquest in the Revolutionary War away from the British in 1779. Greatly disadvantaged in number of troops compared to those inside Fort Sackville, Clark relied on the marksmanship of his troops and the ability to convince the British of a larger army to win the fort. Today the George Rogers Clark National Historical Park in Vincennes is the site of the largest Memorial Monument west of Washington, D.C., which honors the heroic accomplishments of Colonel Clark and his men.

The seal illustrates the Memorial GRC. It is the site of an extremely important battle that occurred which aided the United States in laying claim to the vast region that later became the old northwest territory. Today a massive granite and marble memorial, more than 80 feet high, stands on the Fort Sackville site. Inside is a bronze statue of George Rogers Clark. There are also huge murals around the rotunda and Clark`s words carved into the Indiana limestone.

Feb 25th is recognized by Indiana as George Rogers Clark Day.

# FEBRUARY 26, 1779 - TOWN OF GREENWICH, CT

General Israel Putnam was a hero of the French and Indian Wars. Born in 1718, he was already 57 by the time he participated in the Battle of Bunker Hill. Valued by Washington, he commanded the defense of the vital Hudson River Valley later in the war and Putnam County, New York, is named for him.

General Putnam narrowly avoided capture by the British on February 26, 1779. As is common with legendary stories, General Putnam was either shaving in his home and narrowly escaped or was on the way to Stamford for reinforcements when he was intercepted by British soldiers. Either way ends the same. In an instant, Putnam galloped away down a road leading to the edge of a rock cliff. With the British in close pursuit, Putnam had no choice when he reached the top of the precipice: horse and rider leaped over the edge. The British pulled up and fired their pistols at him while he waved his sword defiantly at them.

The seal illustrates General Israel Putnam's daring escape. The town's history dates back to July 18, 1640, when it became the 10th town established in Connecticut.

*The seal of the Town of Greenwich, CT is used with permission from the Town of Greenwich.*

# JULY 5, 1779 - TOWN OF EAST HAVEN CT

### Black Rock Fort

Here on July 5, 1779, eighteen men under Lieutenant Daniel Bishop stood in defense of New Haven against a British fleet commanded by Commodore Sir George Collier and land forces commanded by Major General William Tryon. When ammunition ran out the Patriots spiked their guns and withdrew but were soon captured. The British had landed over 1,500 men who set about burning many homes in the town.

*Marquis de LaFayette, General in the Continental Army*
*camped here with 2800 troops enroute to*
*Rhode Island July 26 and 27, 1778.*
This historical marker Dedicated here by the CT Sons of the American Revolution,
General David Humphreys Branch and the East Haven Historical Society 1996.

The Town of East Haven became an incorporated town in May 1785.

A Revolutionary Soldier is displayed prominently on the seal.

# JULY 5, 1779 – CITY OF WEST HAVEN CT

British troops marched through the town on the way to burn New Haven on July 5, 1779. The history of West Haven cannot be told without recalling the Williston incident and British Adjutant Campbell's merciful deed. While trying to escape the British raid in 1779, the Rev. Williston fell and broke his leg. Adjutant Campbell prevented his men from shooting him and, in fact, ordered his surgeon to set the leg. Shortly thereafter, Adjutant Campbell lost his life in the vicinity of Allingtown Hill where a monument to his memory now stands.

Over the early years there was a degree of strife as colonials distrusted the Loyalists in their town to the point where it is recorded that a gentleman from Oyster River shot his British sympathizer neighbor in the leg for his disloyalty to the townspeople. Other sympathizers provided beef and fresh produce for British ships during other landings.

Our city seal bears the image of our Paul Revere, teenage militiaman Thomas Painter, as he spotted invading ships entering the harbor.

# JULY 11, 1779 – CITY OF NORWALK CT

2600 British troops under Major General William Tryon arrived on July 10, 1779, and the next day they almost completely destroyed Norwalk by burning it.

They burned 135 houses, 2 churches, 89 barns, 25 shops, 5 vessels, 4 mills, and all the grain in Norwalk ; only six houses were spared. A monument stands at the corner of East Avenue and Adams Avenue to honor the Norwalk citizens who fought the British. This was called 'The Battle of the Rocks'.

It was the militia from Norwalk that was ridiculed by the British Dr Richard Shuckburgh with the writing of Yankee Doodle Dandy as they marched through Rensselaer on the way to Albany to assist the British during the French and Indian War in the 1750s.

The well on the seal represents the well that ships used to replenish their water in the former City of South Norwalk called Old Well.

# JULY 11, 1779 – TOWN OF TRUMBULL CT

In the summer of 1779, General William Tryon sought to punish Americans by attacking civilian targets in coastal Connecticut with a force of about 2,600 British troops. New Haven was raided on July 5th, Fairfield was raided on the 7th and burned. Norwalk was raided on July 10 and burned on the 11th.

 The Town of Trumbull seal shows a colonial soldier at his hillside lookout scanning the skyline toward Long Island Sound for signs of the British. The seal was adopted at the June 19, 1939, selectmen's meeting.

The town seal is described as follows: …. At the right-hand half is a Revolutionary Infantryman in full uniform, standing at rest and facing the center of the seal, holding his musket by the barrel in his right hand, with the stock of the musket resting on the ground by his right foot. His left thumb is caught under his musket and powder belt as he stands looking over a valley and rolling hills which occupy the lower left-hand side of the seal. Directly in front of the soldier can be seen two (2) spears of mullen plant in full bloom, growing between rocks on a hillside, while in back of him can be seen the head and forequarters of his horse …..

# JULY 15-16, 1779 – TOWN OF STONY POINT NY

**BATTLE OF STONY POINT - General Anthony Wayne and his men attacked a British fortification located on the west bank of the Hudson River about 10 miles south of West Point.** They had been given the password by Black spy Pompey Lamb whom the British trusted since he delivered fruit and vegetables to them.

General Wayne commanded the south column comprised of 700 men from Connecticut, Massachusetts, Virginia, and Pennsylvania. Colonel Richard Butler commanded the north column consisting of 300 soldiers, while the diversionary force had 150 men that were led by Major Hardy Murpree. The garrison was held by about 700 well-armed, well-trained British soldiers equipped with heavy cannon. The Americans attacked with no artillery support and no loaded weapons — just fixed-bayonets. Despite strength in numbers, the only real advantage the Americans had was the element of surprise. Within about a half-hour, the heaviest fighting had ended; by 1 A.M. the fort and garrison were in American hands. It was a genuine victory and morale booster for the Americans despite it being considered a suicide mission by some. The town logo depicts "Mad" Anthony Wayne and 13 stars.

# JULY 22, 1779 – TOWN OF HIGHLAND NY

On July 22, 1779, the Upper Delaware's only major Revolutionary War battle was fought on the plateau above Minisink Ford. The battle was fought between the colonial militia of Goshen who suffered a devastating defeat against a group of Indians and Tories commanded by Mohawk Chieftain Joseph Brant. Lt Col Benjamin Tusten and forty-four militiamen were killed during the battle.

Several initial efforts were made to recover the bodies of the defeated Colonials, but it wasn't until 1822 when an expedition was sent out from Goshen to recover the skeletons. The remains of the fallen militiamen were buried in Goshen on July 22, 1822, with a ceremony that was witnessed by an estimated 12,000 people.

Although the Battle of Minisink was an Indian/Tory victory, Washington's troops under the leadership of General John Sullivan advanced into Western New York and eventually defeated the Indians and destroyed their settlements.

The seal is an illustration of an eagle soaring peacefully over the Delaware River near where the Battle of Minisink was fought.

# AUGUST 13, 1779 – CHEMUNG COUNTY NY

The Battle of Chemung took place on August 13, 1779. The Sullivan Expedition destroyed two Indian villages known as Old Chemung and New Chemung. Fifty or sixty houses were destroyed here.

The American invasion resulted in the destruction of forty Indian towns and agricultural fields yielding some 160,000 bushels of corn and other vegetables before returning to the Main Army. Sullivan's army had "chastised" the forces of the Six Nations that were hostile to the United States for taking the side of the British and forever ended the Iroquois Confederacy's military dominance over other Indian nations. Although the British and Iroquois remained allies, the British supply system was indeed strained to support the Indians in their distress.

Chemung County was named for the villages of that name. The seal reflects the Revolutionary history of the county with 13 stars and the American eagle.

# AUGUST 29, 1779 – TOWN OF ASHLAND NY

On this date, the Battle of Newtown was fought on a part of the Town of Ashland.

Gen Sullivan and the 2300 Americans defeated the 1000 strong Iroquois allies. The town and the crops were then destroyed.

Sullivan's expedition had left Easton, PA, on June 18, 1779, and ended on October 3rd with orders from Washington to destroy the capability of the Iroquois nations (Mohawks, Senecas, Cayugas, and Onondagas) that had sided with the British to terrorize the frontier. The only significant battle was at Newtown.

Over 40 Iroquois villages were destroyed along with thousands of acres of crops during Sullivan's campaign. The result was the end of the Iroquois Confederation.

Illustrated on the seal are Sullivan's monument at the Newtown Battlefield State Park and General John Sullivan and Mohawk Chief Joseph Brandt.

# SEPTEMBER 14, 1779 - TOWN OF LEICESTER NY

In the 1779 western campaign of the Revolutionary War, General Sullivan's army burned and pillaged its way through western New York in pursuit of the Seneca Indians, allies of the British. Outnumbered and outgunned, the Senecas made a stand at Little Beard's Town (now the Village of Cuylerville) in the Town of Leicester. History states that Lieutenant Thomas Boyd and Sergeant Michael Parker were captured by British soldiers and Seneca Indians. The men were tied to this tree and tortured in an attempt to make them divulge information regarding General Sullivan's plans along with other war plans. The army upon finding the corpses destroyed the town and ventured no further west.

The Tree has been recognized as an historical landmark by the International Society of Arboriculture and the National Arborist Association. There is a New York Historical Plaque at this site. In 1841 the remains of Lt Boyd & Sgt Parker were exhumed and taken to Rochester.

# SEPTEMBER 24, 1779 - VILLAGE OF HORSEHEADS NY

September 24, 1779 - this date hallmarks the time and hallowed ground where lie the true relics and sun-bleached skulls of the American Military Pack horses of the armies of Major-General John Sullivan. After a 450 mile journey the 1200 pack horses had reached the limits of their endurance and hundreds were humanely disposed of.

A few years later the skulls of the horses were arrayed along the trail in defiant fashion by a few returning Native Americans as a gesture that the same fate would be met by any settler should he attempt to homestead on this location. An earlier report indicated a horse's skull on a post was a symbol of a Tory farm. The first settlers, reading these Native American signs, promptly built their homes on the spot.

This location, first known as "The Valley of Horses Heads," was later changed to Horseheads, New York. Horseheads is the first and only town and village in the United States dedicated to the service of the American Military Horse. A twenty-eight square mile memorial, unparalleled in American Military History, is the proud distinction that enshrines the Town and Village of Horseheads, New York.

# OCTOBER 9, 1779 – CITY OF SAVANNAH GA

The British captured Savannah on December 29, 1778. On October 9, 1779, after the Siege of Savannah failed, a combined French and American force of 4500 attacked the 2500 British defenders. The battle turned out to be a disaster and one of the bloodiest in the war with over 800 casualties within an hour. Brig General Casimir Pulaski from Poland was mortally wounded as he commanded soldiers during the attack and eventually died and was buried at sea. Sgt William Jasper, a hero of the Battle of Sullivan's Island SC, in 1776, was also killed while attempting to plant the colors on the redoubt.

Gen Benjamin Lincoln retreated to Charleston where he was defeated and surrendered over 5400 soldiers to the British on May 12, 1780. Savannah remained under British control until 1782.

The seal of the City of Savannah was laid in the center of the floor of City Hall in 1906 in shades of red, white and blue and depicts the scales of Justice, the sword of Truth, and the omniscient eye.

# 1780

May 12 - City of Charleston SC

May 28 – Sumter County SC

May 29 – Lancaster County SC

June 7 – Union County NJ

June 23 – Township of Springfield NJ

August 2 – Fort Plain NY

August – Hart County GA

August 8 – Clark County OH

August 16 – City of Camden SC

September 1 – Town of Rutherfordton NC

September 23 – Village of Tarrytown NY

September 25 – Washington County VA

September 25 – Town of Abingdon VA

September 25 – City of Elizabethton TN

September 26 – City of Charlotte NC

September 30 – Town of Wilkesboro NC

September 30 – City of Morganton NC

October 7 – City of Kings Mountain NC

October 17 – Village of Middleburg NY

October 19 – County of Montgomery NY

Oct ober 23 – Borough of Woodland Park NJ

November 8 – City of Manning SC

Quotes on Timothy Murphy

# MAY 12, 1780 – CITY OF CHARLESTON SC

In late 1779, the British launched an attack against Charles Town with 14,000 troops. General Washington sends more than 1,000 Continentals to help defend the city. British warships penetrate the forts guarding the harbor entrance and the British Army initiates a 40-day siege to the city in March of 1780.

Ultimately, General Benjamin Lincoln surrendered Charles Town and 5400 soldiers to the British on May 12, who occupied the city for more than two years. Many prominent citizens are targeted and arrested for promoting resistance. To gain their release, they must agree to sign an Oath of Loyalty to the Crown.

In late 1781 American forces retake most of South Carolina. When the victory reaches London, Britain resolves to end the war. On December 14, 1782, the defeated British Army leaves Charles Town, bringing the occupation to a close.

The seal since 1783 portrays a seated woman with scepter pointed toward the mouth of the harbor, against a background of the city skyline, with a full-rigged sailing vessel making for port and the motto, "AEDES MORES JURAQUE CURAT" which translates (she cares for her temples, customs and rights).

# MAY 28, 1780 – SUMTER COUNTY SC

Sumter County, SC, and its County seat, the City of Sumter, were named for Revolutionary War General Thomas Sumter (1734-1832), who was a resident of the area.

He was effectively out of the war until May 28, 1780, when he learned that Col Banastre Tarleton was on the way to arrest him. His house was burned while his wife was forced to watch. Later, in November of 1780, Gen Sumter defeated Banastre which contributed to the British leaving the Carolinas for Virginia.

His fighting style led Cornwallis to refer to him as "fighting like a gamecock."

Sumter served as one of several figures for the lead character in the movie "The Patriot" that was released in 2000.

# MAY 29, 1780 – LANCASTER COUNTY SC

Col Buford's 11th Virginia Regiment and a detachment of Washington's Cavalry retreating after the fall of Charles Town SC, were attacked by Col Tarleton, May 29, 1780, at the site of the monument 955 feet southwest. The American loss was 113 killed, 150 wounded, 53 made prisoner; the British, 5 killed, 14 wounded….

Among the nurses tending to the wounded was Elizabeth Jackson and her thirteen year old son, Andrew (who would become our 7th President). He was scarred for life by a British officer's sword for refusing to clean his boots while a prisoner in 1781.

Before the massacre, popular opinion held that the Southern states were lost to the Patriot cause and would remain loyal to Britain. The reports of the Waxhaw Massacre, however, may have changed the direction of the war in the South. Many who might have stayed neutral flocked to the Patriots. The massacre was also directly responsible for the over-mountain men forming a volunteer force that utterly destroyed Major Patrick Ferguson's command at Kings Mountain, South Carolina.

## JUNE 7, 1780 - UNION COUNTY NJ

On June 7, 1780, British Troops passed the Presbyterian parsonage at Connecticut Farms (now Union). A shot was fired through a window and Hannah Caldwell, wife of the "Fighting Parson" James Caldwell, fell dead.

The event is depicted on the Union County seal. The British burned the church and the parsonage, which was rebuilt two years later on the old foundation. Today, the parsonage is a repository of furniture, clothing, personal effects, archival materials and other artifacts related to Union Township's history from the 18th century through the early 20th century.

The battle that followed was the last battle in the North and is sometimes referred to as the "Forgotten Battle."

# JUNE 23, 1780 - TOWNSHIP OF SPRINGFIELD NJ

Washington had his General Headquarters in Springfield from June 7-22, 1780. On June 23, 1780, "The Battle of Springfield" was fought. The British advanced with infantry, cavalry and several field pieces. During the heat of the battle, Reverend James Caldwell, Chaplain of Colonel Elias Dayton's Regiment, whose wife had been murdered 16 days before, passed out Watts Hymnals from the Presbyterian Church for use as wadding. His cry of "Give Them Watts, Boys" has lived on to become a Motto of that conflict. The seal is a Continental soldier surrounded by 13 stars.

During the fighting in the Revolutionary War, the enemy entered the town a number of times to take away farm animals, grain and other needs, keeping the people in a continual state of alarm. It became necessary for the local populace to set up a chain of signals. When necessary, a cannon called "Old Sow" was fired to alert our militia on both sides of the mountain and to warn the people to flee to a place of safety.

*The Township of Springfield seal is used with permission of the Township of Springfield.*

**OLD BLOCK HOUSE
OF FORT PLAIN**

# AUGUST 2, 1780 – VILLAGE OF FORT PLAIN NY

The Fort Plain section was devastated and 16 people were killed and 60 captured during a great raid of Tories and Indians under Joseph Brant on Aug. 2, 1780.

The local militia had gone up the river convoying supplies when the red and white savages broke from the woods. A woman fired the signal gun at the fort warning the scattered settlers to take to the bush or woods or to run for the nearest blockhouse. Many gathered in Fort Plain and, fearing an attack, the women there donned men's hats and took poles and guns, showing themselves sufficiently above the palisades to give the impression of a large garrison. The ruse was successful as the savages avoided the fortification. This was referred to as "Manning the Fort."

This logo is used on the Village stationery.

## AUGUST 1780 - HART COUNTY GA

The most famous story about Nancy Hart occurred during the Revolutionary War when seven British (or Loyalist) soldiers arrived at her cabin near Wahatchie Creek. Her normal hostility toward the British was replaced that day by a cordial manner, and she offered the soldiers a meal. The British soldiers began to drink while Nancy kept an eye on them and their muskets that were carelessly stacked in the corner. Nancy managed to sneak two of the muskets into a space in the wall before she was noticed trying to sneak the remainder. One of the soldiers rushed at her but she was an expert marksman and dropped him to the floor. Another soldier followed and was injured by Nancy's excellent shot. When her husband Benjamin and his friends arrived at the cabin, Nancy had the five enemy soldiers and the situation under control. The soldiers were hanged from an old oak tree and buried on the Harts' farm. The grave was unearthed by a work crew when building the railroad, verifying the history which had been considered by many to be mere legend.

A representation of Nancy Hart above the Hartwell Dam may be seen on the Hart County Seal. Designed by Robert W. Knowles, it was adopted on May 8, 1990. Hart County is the only county in GA named for a woman.

# AUGUST 8, 1780 - CLARK COUNTY OH

Approximately three miles west of Springfield at the present site of George Rogers Clark Memorial Park lay the Shawnee Indian Town called Piqua. This town was the site of the Battle of Piqua on August 8th, 1780 - one of the last battles of the American Revolution in the West.

Gen George Rogers Clark with his Kentucky soldiers defeated and drove from this area the Shawnee Indians thus aiding to make the Northwest Territory part of the United States. The battle was a significant one in the struggle of the pioneer for the West and in the struggle of the American colonies for ascendancy over the British during the American Revolution. The permanent settlement of the area of Ohio began within a decade and a half after Gen Clark's victory.

A larger-than-life Brigadier General George Rogers Clark on the bank of the Mad River and his cabin are illustrated on the seal. November 19th is designated as George Rogers Clark Day in Ohio in honor of his birthday in 1752.

## AUGUST 16, 1780 - CITY OF CAMDEN SC

In May of 1780 the American Revolution returned to Charleston. It fell and Lord Charles Cornwallis and 2,500 British troops immediately marched to Camden and set up the main British supply post for the Southern Campaign. For eleven months the citizens of Camden understood the atrocities of war.

Two battles were fought nearby. The Battle of Camden, the worst American battle defeat of the Revolution, was fought on August 16, 1780, nine miles north of the museum. Gen Gates, the hero of Saratoga, fled the battlefield and was never a factor in the war again. This was a low point for the patriots.

Nearby, Gen Nathanael Greene and approximately 1,400 Americans engaged 950 British soldiers commanded by Lord Francis Rawdon on April 25, 1781, at Hobkirk's Hill. It was a costly British win and forced the Redcoats to evacuate Camden.

# SEPTEMBER 1, 1780 - TOWN OF RUTHERFORDTON NC

Rutherfordton replaced the small village of Gilbert Town (once located 3 miles north). British Maj Ferguson arrived at Gilbert Town September 1, 1780, and set up camp there. Ferguson used William Gilbert's home. His troops camped on the high hill behind the Gilbert house and the hill is still known as "Ferguson's Hill."

Ferguson had paroled a captured rebel from Gilbert Town and sent him with a message, *"that if they did not desist from their opposition to the British arms, and take protection under his standard, he would march his army over the mountains, hang their leaders, and lay their country waste with fire and sword."*

The soldier represents Brig Gen Griffith Rutherford, hero of the Revolutionary War. Gen Rutherford participated in Ramseurs Mill, the Siege of Charlestown and was wounded at the Battle of Camden.

## SEPTEMBER 23, 1780 – VILLAGE OF TARRYTOWN NY

On September 23, 1780, Major John Andre was captured by three local New York militiamen, John Paulding, David Williams and Isaac Van Wert. In his boot were the stolen plans of West Point that Andre was carrying to the British for traitor Benedict Arnold. Many historians consider this capture to be a major turning point of the Revolution.

The plans were turned over to Lt Col John Jameson from Culpeper, Virginia who did not trust his superior, Gen Benedict Arnold, so Jameson sent the papers directly to George Washington. The plot was uncovered but Benedict Arnold escaped.

On October 2, 1780, Major Andre was hanged.

The seal depicts the discovery of the plans and the capture of the spy, Major Andre.

# SEPTEMBER 25, 1780 - WASHINGTON COUNTY VA

The message sent over the mountains by British Maj Ferguson had the reverse effect. Instead of intimidating the local population, they decided to challenge him and the loyalists he was leading before they arrived.

In the fall of 1780, four hundred men from Washington County were mustered to travel under the command of Col William Campbell. Col John Sevier also gathered his men to respond to the challenge from Ferguson.

Washington County was formed in 1776 and named for General George Washington before he was elected President. The seal is taken from the Washington family coat-of-arms. The seal was designed by Arthur DuBois, a well known authority on heraldry and seals and was adopted by the Board of Supervisors on January 4, 1978.

# SEPTEMBER 25, 1780 – TOWN OF ABINGDON VA

In September of 1780, Col William Campbell's regiment mustered at Black's Fort in Washington County, then joined Tennessee regiments at Watauga Shoals in the first Volunteer military expedition. Joseph Black was a Lieutenant in Captain Dysart's company of the Campbell regiment.

In 1771 or 1772 Joseph Black moved to Beaver Creek at Wolf Hills where he was one of the founding members of Sinking Springs Presbyterian Church. In 1774 he built Black's Fort capable of sheltering up to 600 settlers. Black's Fort became the county seat of the newly formed Washington County Virginia in 1776. In 1778 Black's Fort was renamed Abingdon after Martha Custis Washington's English manor.

The seal has an illustration of Black's Fort where the soldiers mustered for the march south.

# SEPTEMBER 25, 1780 –CITY OF ELIZABETHTON, TN

On September 25, militia Col Isaac Shelby and militia Col John Sevier gathered at Sycamore Shoals with over 400 men. Col William and Arthur Campbell of Virginia arrived with an additional 400 riflemen. A unit of some 160 Old Burke militiamen was already camped in the area with their leader, Col Charles McDowell. Now numbering more than 900 strong, the Sycamore Shoals militiamen marched south on September 26.

Here was established one of the earliest permanent American settlements beyond the mountains and the Watauga Association , the first majority-rule system of American democratic government was formed in 1772.

The seal reflects the minuteman statue against the American Flag and the mountains of Tennessee.

# SEPTEMBER 26, 1780 – CITY OF CHARLOTTE NC

Independent of Ferguson, on September 26, 1780, Gen Charles Cornwallis rode into Charlotte. Flushed with the victory in Camden, he was directed to subdue the Carolinas. Expecting a welcome from Loyalists, he instead was greeted with Patriot gunfire, prompting the comparison to a hornet's nest – Charlotte's symbol since then.

The tree represents growth. A hornet's nest can be seen on the left tree branch. The hornet's nest has long been a symbol for Charlotte, because in the American Revolution, her citizens fought so fiercely that a British general compared being in Charlotte to being in a hornet's nest. A Liberty cap, such as the kind worn by patriots from the area during the Revolution, hangs from the right tree branch. The hands signify friendship, and the year, 1775, is when the Mecklenburg Declaration of Independence was signed.

# SEPTEMBER 30, 1780 – TOWN OF WILKESBORO NC

For two and a half centuries the Tory Oak grew strong and stately in the center of Wilkesboro, a symbol of the revolutionary struggle that led to the founding of our country. Some leaders called this old tree the Liberty Oak, but it became famous because Tories were hanged on its limbs when the tree was still young.

No great Revolutionary War battles were fought in Wilkesboro. Instead of a battlefield with monuments, the Tory Oak became the proud local symbol of the successful War for American Independence.

Members of the militia, sometimes known as Mountain Men, were ordinary working citizens. According to legend, local resident Col Benjamin Cleveland climbed atop nearby Rendezvous Mountain and blew his powder horn to summon over 200 militiamen. They joined the Overmountain Men and he was one of the commanders at the Battle of Kings Mountain. He took the British Major Patrick Ferguson's white horse as his "war prize" and in compensation for the loss of his own horse during that battle.

# SEPTEMBER 30, 1780 – CITY OF MORGANTON NC

This impressive number of 900 arrived at Joseph McDowell's Quaker Meadows farm on September 30, 1780. On the same day they were joined by Col Benjamin Cleveland from Wilkesboro and Joseph Winston from Surry with an additional 350 men.

The combined forces camped at Quaker Meadows now totaled almost 1,400 men. That evening the leaders, all colonels, met in council under a handsome, wide-branching oak tree in a nearby field to discuss their plans. As history records, it was these "barbarians" (as British Major Ferguson named them) who then ambled southward from Quaker Meadows to meet their destiny at the Battle of Kings Mountain on October 7, 1780.

Morganton was named for Revolutionary War hero Brig Gen Daniel Morgan. It would be in January of 1781 when Morgan won an important battle at Cowpens SC.

The seal is a view of Pilot Mountain that the army passed as it left Quaker Meadow on the way to Gilbert's Town (now Rutherfordton).

## OCTOBER 7, 1780 – CITY OF KINGS MOUNTAIN NC

The American forces were militia groups who soundly defeated the Loyalists under Maj Patrick Ferguson. He was killed on the field of battle that lasted about an hour. Among the Mountain Men who fought there was John Crockett, father of future patriot, Davy Crockett.  Over 200 Loyalist soldiers were killed and 700 taken prisoner.

This battle was very important in early American history, being later proclaimed "the turning point of the American Revolution in the South" by President Andrew Jackson. This victory ended the British plan for invasion of North Carolina and was a great morale booster for the Americans after a series of defeats. Cornwallis had to abandon his plans to conquer North Carolina.

Incorporated on February 11, 1874, Kings Mountain takes its name from the historical Revolutionary battle fought five miles South (in South Carolina), thus bringing meaning to our motto "The Historical City."

The seal is an illustration of the monument at Kings Mountain National Park in SC.

# OCTOBER 17, 1780 – VILLAGE OF MIDDLEBURGH NY

The Schoharie valley was known as the "Breadbasket of the Revolution" and was protected in part by the "Middle Fort" in what is now Middleburgh. In 1777 during the American Revolution, the Middle Fort was constructed about three quarters of a mile north of the village.

On October 15, Col Sir John Johnson led a force of 800-1,500 British regulars, Tories, and Indians to the Susquehanna River in the Schoharie Valley. Along the way they burned all of the local farms as they passed them. Records indicate that a strong northeast wind aided the torch when the British set fire to all the buildings and crops. Cattle were either killed or driven away, and the best horses were appropriated by the British.

Here, Timothy Murphy defied the Fort's Commander, Major Woolsey, when he was ready to surrender. The Colonials rallied and the fort was successfully defended against the British and Indian allies on October 17, 1780.

The illustration is of the Middle Fort from the Village website
Information courtesy of Charlie Spickerman, Local Historian

# OCTOBER 19, 1780 - COUNTY OF MONTGOMERY NY

The Revolutionary War had significant impact upon the residents of Montgomery County. Four regiments, consisting of enlisted men throughout the valley, made up the Tryon County militia. Blood was shed on the lands within the county during this time. The Battles of Klock's Field and Stone Arabia that took place on October 19 wreaked havoc. Lives and homes of area residents were ravaged and terrorized by groups that included their former neighbors.

Tryon County was renamed Montgomery County on April 2, 1784. Brig Gen Richard Montgomery was killed in battle in Quebec in 1775. His wife would never remarry and would outlive him by 53 years. She always referred to him as "my soldier."

Montgomery County was first named Tryon County in 1772 after then NY Royal Governor William Tryon.

# OCTOBER 23, 1780 - BOROUGH OF WOODLAND PARK NJ

On Rifle Camp Road, just off of Route 46, is a historic marker that reads:
*"Great Notch - Used by Washington as a lookout while quartered at the Dey House, October 1780. Major Parr's Rifle Corps camped in ravine ."*

The idea for the design was inspired by the nation's bicentennial in 1976 but not completed until 1996. George Galbraith's concept was completed with the assistance of a local art class at Passaic Valley High School.

West Paterson's name was changed to the Borough of Woodland Park, effective January 1, 2009.

# NOVEMBER 8, 1780 - CITY OF MANNING SC

November 8, 1780 - Upon learning from a Tory spy that General Francis Marion slipped back east of Jack's Creek, Tarleton gave chase with the Green Dragoons. Marion, staying just ahead of the dragoons, and fighting a series of delaying actions finally slipped away into Ox Swamp. Here Tarleton gave up the chase and said "as for the old fox, the devil himself could not catch him." Ox Swamp is just east of Manning. Thus, General Marion became known as the *"Swamp Fox."* General Marion participated in several more battles throughout 1780 and 1781. He died on Feb 27th, 1795. Feb 27th has been enacted as General Francis Marion Memorial Day.

The City of Manning was established in 1856 as the county seat for the newly formed Clarendon County. The city is named for John Laurence Manning (1816 - 1889). John Laurence Manning was elected to both chambers in the General Assembly and served as governor from 1852 to 1854.

The seal depicts a cannon and a Palmetto Tree.

# REVOLUTIONARY WAR HERO TIMOTHY MURPHY

The following is from the 1929 dedication address of the state monument by then New York Governor Franklin Delano Roosevelt.

"This country has been made by Timothy Murphys, the men in the ranks. Conditions here called for the qualities of the heart and head that Tim Murphy had in abundance. Our histories should tell us more of the men in the ranks, for it was to them, more than to the generals, that we were indebted for our military victories."

A bronze plaque on the New York grave of Murphy states,

"Tim Murphy - Patriot, Soldier, Scout, Citizen who served distinguishably in Morgan's Rifle Corps, fought at Saratoga and Monmouth and whose bravery repelled the attack of the British and their Indian allies from Middlefort, October 17, 1780 and saved the lives of the colonists of his Schoharie Valley. Here too, this warrior sire, with honor rests who braved in freedom's cause his valiant breast."

# 1781

February 12 – Town Of Summerfield NC

March 15 – City Of Greensboro NC

March 15 – County Of Guilford NC

April  - Town Of Liberty NC

April 25 – Town Of Petersburg VA

May 21 – Town Of Wethersfield CT

June 4 – City Of Charlottesville VA

June 5 – Fluvanna County VA

July 1 – Town of Southbury CT

August 18 – Town Of Greenburgh NY

August 21 – Town of Yorktown NY

August 29 – Town Of Elizabethtown NC

September 6 – City Of Groton CT

September 6 – Town Of Groton CT

September 6 – City Of New London CT

October 19 – County Of York VA

# FEBRUARY 12, 1781 - TOWN OF SUMMERFIELD NC

Summerfield, settled by English colonists in the 1700s, once was called Bruce's Cross Roads. It was named for Charles Bruce, who built a large plantation near the intersection of two early stagecoach routes.

As a supporter of the Continental Army during the Revolutionary War, Bruce oversaw munitions for the patriots. Thus, in the winter of 1781, it was to Bruce's home that Colonel Light Horse Harry Lee (a military hero and father of Robert E. Lee) rode with his men to seek refuge as they evaded British forces.

It was at a skirmish with the British in the vicinity of Bruce's Cross Roads that Light-Horse Lee's bugler boy, James Gilles, gave up his life. Gilles, whose image graces the town seal, is buried in the Bruce family cemetery, a landmark of the community.

Returning north from his "Southern Tour," in 1791, George Washington is said to have stopped at State Senator Bruce's home.

# MARCH 15, 1781 - CITY OF GREENSBORO NC

Greensboro is named after General Nathanael Greene of the Revolutionary War and Commander of the Continental Army at the Battle of Guilford Courthouse fought inside the present city limits of Greensboro on March 15, 1781.

"We fight, get beat, rise, and fight again," – Gen Greene.

The official city seal is a replica of the statue of General Greene surrounded by an oak leaf wreath. The oak leaf is symbolic of sturdiness and durability. In 1808, Greensboro received its corporate charter from the North Carolina General Assembly.

The seal has been in use for decades: however, there are no records available that determine when the seal was adopted.

## MARCH 15, 1781 - COUNTY OF GUILFORD NC

The Battle of Guilford Courthouse was fought on March 15, 1781. One hero of that day was Peter Francisco. March 15th is observed as Peter Francisco day in Massachusetts, Virginia and Rhode Island. Wounded over 6 times in the war, Washington referred to him as a "One-Man Army".

In 1981, the Board of County Commissioners adopted the official seal for Guilford County. The elements of the coat-of-arms come from the arms of

> Dr. David Caldwell, prominent educator, minister, physician, statesman and patriot;
> General Nathanael Greene, commander of colonial troops at the Revolutionary Battle of Guilford Courthouse;
> and the first and second Earls of Guilford, for whom the County was named.

From the Greene arms come the buck of the supporters and the buck's head on the shield.

# APRIL 1781 – TOWN OF LIBERTY NC

The Town of Liberty, once part of Orange County, and later Guilford County would eventually become part of Randolph County after succession in 1779. During the war soldiers camped out in what is now Liberty. A large Oak tree in the center of the camp was used as a make shift town square, meeting place, and ultimately a place to hang war time criminals. The Soldiers called it the Liberty Oak, after the Boston "Liberty Tree" a national symbol of individual Liberty & Anti-Tyranny; popularized by the "Sons of Liberty."

Sometime in the Spring of 1781, probably April, and probably in Randolph County, Capt David Fanning and his men were surrounded at a house of a friend by 14 whig militia under a Capt. Hinds, with both sides losing a man killed. Fanning and most of his men apparently were forced to retreat and made their escape. One of Fanning's men was captured by Hinds, and says Fanning in his Narrative, hanged "on the spot where we had killed the man [a whig] a few days before".

# APRIL 25, 1781 – TOWN OF PETERSBURG VA

The British army, under the command of Major General William Phillips, landed at City Point (now Hopewell) on April 24th. The Virginia militia was commanded by Brigadier General Peter Muhlenberg under the overall command of Major General Frederick Willhelm von Steuben.

Outnumbered by the British army of 2,500 to the militia strength of barely over 1,000 men, the Virginians denied the King's soldiers the opportunity of capturing the city without fighting for it. Most history books list the action at Petersburg as a minor battle or skirmish. However, the stand of the Americans against such an overwhelming force was a full-scale battle by any Revolutionary War standards. The battle actually bought a full day's time for Lafayette to entrench his army on the heights of Richmond, and ultimately prevented a second "sacking" of Richmond.

The British retreated toward Yorktown where they ultimately surrendered in Oct.

This seal illustrates the port of Petersburg prior to its incorporation as a town in 1848.

SEAL

PORT of DISTRIBUTION to the INTERIOR 1634-1800-CHARTERED 1662-PATENT 1686-INC.1822. WETHERSFIELD, CONNECTICUT

# MAY 21, 1781 - TOWN OF WETHERSFIELD CT

Wethersfield, founded in 1633-34, has its niche in history, being "Ye Most Auncient Towne" in Connecticut, as set out by the Code of 1650 - "Colonial Records of Connecticut." Here on May 21, 1781, at the Joseph Webb House on Main Street, Generals Washington and Rochambeau planned the Battle of Yorktown, which culminated in the independence of the then rebellious colonies.

Silas Deane, member of the Continental Congress in 1774 and 1775, and regarded as America's first diplomat, hosted George Washington at his home in Wethersfield during Washington's first visit to town in 1775.

Wethersfield's Town Seal was designed by Jared Standish. The design in the central disk features the Cove Warehouse. Shown around the Warehouse are a girl, carrying a bag of the Wethersfield Red Onions which were shipped around the world, two native Americans, and a ship being built. The existing Cove Warehouse is maintained as a museum property by the Wethersfield Historical Society.

# JUNE 4, 1781 - CITY OF CHARLOTTESVILLE VA

Highway marker Inscription  - "On 4 June 1781, John "Jack" Jouett Jr. arrived at the Albemarle County Courthouse to warn the Virginia legislature of approaching British troops. The state government under Governor Thomas Jefferson had retreated from Richmond to reconvene in Charlottesville because of the threat of British invasion during the Revolutionary War. Jouett had spotted Colonel Banastre Tarleton and his 180 dragoons and 70 cavalrymen 40 miles east at Cuckoo Tavern, and rode through the night to reach here by dawn. Jouett's heroic ride, which allowed Jefferson and all but seven of the legislators to escape, was later recognized by the Virginia General Assembly, which awarded him a sword and a pair of pistols. "

One of the seven legislators detained was Daniel Boone.

The seal or logo of Charlottesville was designed by Mr. R. W. Vanderberry in June 1971.  The seal is divided into four quadrants illustrating the Rotunda of the University of Virginia designed by Thomas Jefferson, a dogwood blossom, a cannon and the entrance to City Hall.

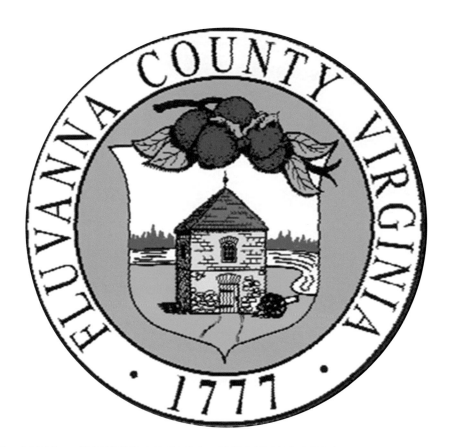

# JUNE 5, 1781 – FLUVANNA COUNTY VA

Fluvanna County was established in 1777 from Albemarle County and was named for the Fluvanna River which in turn was named for the Queen of England as "Annes" River.

Fluvanna was defended by six militia companies and Continental Army troops during the Revolution. The county was invaded by British forces and the Point of Forks Arsenal was burned as a result of the Battle of Point of Forks on June 5, 1781.

Fluvanna County is diagonally bisected by the Rivanna River. The tan represents the leading industry of the county – farming and timber. Fluvanna is often called the "Persimmon County". Persimmons were once an integral part of Fluvanna pride. The seal contains a branch of persimmons at the top of the interior crest.

The Point of Fork Arsenal pictured on the shield was one of Virginia's principal military arsenals during and after the Revolution.

# JULY 1, 1781 – TOWN OF SOUTHBURY CT

In July 1781, Gen Count de Rochambeau and his French troops marched through Southbury to join General Washington. It is said that some camped in the White Oak section.

Shadrack Osborne operated a military commissary for the colony on what is now known as Main Street North near the churches, and issued provisions to many troops passing through town. During the Revolutionary War years and after the capture of Danbury, Shadrack Osborne as head of the commissary, hid hundreds of barrels of pork in a hollow, located about 1 mile southeast of the UCC Church. That area is still called "Pork Hollow". Bullet Hill School was built and named for a hill near it used for firing practice during the Revolutionary War. It was said that bullets were melted down in a fireplace at the school to be used again, and that women cast bullets for the army.

Southbury is the only town in the country with that name. The town seal reads "Unica Unaque," meaning "The One and Only."

# AUGUST 18, 1781 – TOWN OF GREENBURGH NY

Greenburgh was the location of the Philipsburg Encampment from July 6th through August 18-19th, 1781. This included the adjoining camps of the American and French forces under Washington and Rochambeau. The encampment covered a large area on both sides of Sprain Brook in what is now Unincorporated Greenburgh and the northern part of Ardsley.

In effect, it became the staging ground for the final march to Virginia and the decisive Siege of Yorktown there.

The seal illustrates a typical Colonial era campfire for soldiers.

# AUGUST 21, 1781 – TOWN OF YORKTOWN NY

The Town of Yorktown, New York was settled in 1683 and incorporated in 1788. Yorktown was named in commemoration of America's decisive Revolutionary War victory at Yorktown, Virginia.

On August 21, 1781, The French forces under Comte de Rochambeau camped in the surrounding area of Hunt's Tavern (Route 202 corner of Hallocks Mill Rd) on their way to fight the British at Yorktown, Virginia. On August 22nd, they marched from Crompound (Yorktown) to Verplank and then crossed the Hudson River at King's Ferry. In 1782, they camped in Yorktown again on the return trip.
— source Highway Marker.

The seal was the result of a contest for the Bicentennial sponsored by the local Jaycees. No records exist for the special significance of the seal.

# AUGUST 29, 1781 - TOWN OF ELIZABETHTOWN NC

In 1781, patriot forces in the Cape Fear area were in turmoil. The only regular military force for either side was Major James Craig's British garrison at Wilmington. After Cornwallis marched north into Virginia, Craig set in motion a daring plan in which he utilized loyalist militia to wrest control of the colony from rebel forces. This move by the canny British commander resulted in some of the bloodiest fighting of the war, in what was essentially a civil war. In Bladen County, Highland Scots and others loyal to the British all but destroyed the opposing rebel forces there.

Here sixty men, driven from their homes, their estates ravaged and houses plundered, who had taken refuge with the rebel forces, without funds and bare clothing, resolved to return, fight, conquer, or die. They took on a larger force of 300 men and so thoroughly defeated them that the Tories were never a factor again. Patriot prisoners at Elizabethtown were freed after the battle.

The seal is a stylized patriot militia soldier who won the Battle of Elizabethtown.

# SEPTEMBER 6, 1781 – CITY OF GROTON CT

The seal shows an illustration of the monument dedicated to those who sacrificed their lives in 1781. This granite monument was dedicated in 1830 to the men who had defended Fort Griswold.

Late that summer, the British generals were anxious to distract Washington who was then marching south. They decided to create a diversion by attacking an important northern supply center, New London, and, with the same stroke, destroy the "Rebel pirate ships." The command of the expedition fell to Benedict Arnold who had deserted the American cause the year before, and who, being a native of nearby Norwich, knew the harbor area well. 1700 British attacked 164 Americans and killed 85 even after they tried to surrender.

# SEPTEMBER 6, 1781 – TOWN OF GROTON CT

During the American Revolution the town was active against the tyranny of King George, sending out privateers to prey on British commerce. Perhaps in reprisal for their success, superior troops led by the traitor Benedict Arnold attacked Fort Griswold on Groton Heights Sept. 6, 1781. The one-sided battle ended with a dreadful massacre of the brave American defenders. The site is marked with a 134-foot monument and is now Fort Griswold Battlefield State Park.

Groton was settled by John Winthrop, Jr. in 1646 to found Pequot Plantation. Groton was named in honor of the Winthrop estate in England.

Groton became known as the Submarine Capital of the World when the Electric Boat Division of General Dynamics delivered 74 diesel submarines to the Navy in World War II. This was followed in 1954 with the launch of the USS Nautilus, the world's first nuclear-powered submarine, now permanently berthed at Goss Cove near the Submarine Base.

## SEPTEMBER 6, 1781 – CITY OF NEW LONDON CT

The harbor was considered to be the best deep water harbor on Long Island Sound and consequently New London became a base of American naval operations during the Revolutionary War. Famous New Londoners during the American Revolution include Nathan Hale, William Coit, Richard Douglass, Thomas & Nathaniel Shaw, Gen Samuel Parsons, Printer Timothy Green and Reverend Seabury. New London was raided & nearly burned to the ground on September 6, 1781, Battle of Groton Heights, by Norwich Native Benedict Arnold in the attempts to destroy the colonial privateer fleet and storage of goods and naval stores within the city.

The seal is an illustration of an American flagged, full rigged ship with the banner "MARE LIBERIUM" or "Free Seas."

# SEPTEMBER 27, 1781 - TOWN OF DUMFRIES VA

In September, General Washington and French Lt Gen Rochambeau and their armies encamped in Dumfries on their way to victory in Yorktown. In July 1782, they encamped in Dumfries again on their return to NY. – source Highway Marker.

The Town Seal was designed by Mr. Lee Lansing, Town Historian, and adopted by the Town Council in 1978. The elements of the seal are contained within the pattern formed by the outer frame of a hawser rope or cable, and the inner frame of an anchor chain, of a type employed in ships of the Colonial era. The thistle indicates the Scottish founders of the town, with the name of Dumfries, taken by John Graham, the founder, in honor of his home in Scotland.

The supporters of the shield are, on the left, a Piscataway brave, of the Powhatan Confederacy, the predominant tribe along the Potomac, in this area. On the right, a Colonial militiaman of 1775, when Colonel Henry Lee was company Commander. Col Harry Lee was at the Battles of Germantown, Paulus Springs and Eutaw Springs. He is also the father of Robert E. Lee.

# OCTOBER 19, 1781 – COUNTY OF YORK VA

Present at the surrender of Cornwallis' Army of 6000-8000 British soldiers was Marquis de Lafayette, Peter Francisco, Lt Gen Rochambeau, Maj Gen Benjamin Lincoln and some 17,000 American and French soldiers in addition to Washington. This effectively ended the Revolutionary War.

The ship in the seal represents the early settlement of the County by way of the York River. The cannon and flags represent the Revolutionary War battle that took place in and around Yorktown in 1781. The battle in which the American and allied forces were victorious over the British, is recognized as one of the turning points in the history of our nation and the world. Of the three flags shown, the American and French are in the most important positions and the British flag is shown furled to indicate the removal of British authority from the colonies. The "Monument to Alliance and Victory" is the most prominent feature of the seal. The Monument was authorized by Congress on October 29, 1781, just 10 days after the surrender.

The seal was first presented to the Board of Supervisors in 1969 by its designer, Charles Waddell.

# 1782

| | |
|---|---|
| April 16, 1782 | City Of Newburgh NY |
| May 20, 1782 | Town Of Plympton MA |
| June 20, 1782 | Official Seal of the United States |
| September 11, 1782 | City of Wheeling WV |

# 1783

| | |
|---|---|
| April 19, 1783 | Town Of New Windsor NY |
| November 25, 1783 | New York City |

# APRIL 16, 1782 - CITY OF NEWBURGH NY

On April 16, 1782, Washington established the headquarters of the Army at Newburgh.   A strategic spot for the defense of the young nation, Newburgh has been called the "birthplace of the republic." General Washington not only guided the war from here but kept the dream of a republic alive by quelling a military rebellion and probable martial law and refusing to accept a crown as America's first king.

The British were still in New York and skirmishes continued while peace negotiations dragged on. Washington made his headquarters in the last year and a half of the war at the home of the Hasbrouck family, which in 1850 became the first building bought by a state to be preserved as an historic site. The house is now on the seal of the City of Newburgh.

It was also while based in Newburgh that Washington first awarded the Badge of Merit, later known as the Purple Heart. The first three known recipients were Sgt Elijah Churchill, 2nd Continental Dragoons; Sgt William Brown and Sgt Daniel Bissel, 2nd Connecticut Continental Line Infantry.

- The seal of the City of Newburgh is used with the permission of the City of Newburgh.

## MAY 20, 1782 - TOWN OF PLYMPTON MA

Inspired by the writings of Thomas Paine, on May 20, 1782, when she was twenty-one, Deborah Sampson enlisted in the Fourth Massachusetts Regiment of the Continental Army at Bellingham as a man named Robert Shurtleff (also listed as Shirtliff or Shirtlieff). On May 23rd, she was mustered into service at Worcester. Being 5 foot 7 inches tall, she looked tall for a woman and she had bound her breasts tightly to approximate a male physique. She performed her duties as well as any other man.

She was wounded on July 2, 1782 in Tarrytown NY, but refused treatment for two musket balls in her thigh for fear she would be discovered. Her secret was subsequently discovered while she was serving in Philadelphia where she was ill with fever. She was honorably discharged on October 25, 1783. She received a pension and was an acquaintance and friend of Paul Revere.

Deborah Sampson was born in Plympton on December 17, 1760. She ultimately married and bore three children.

# JUNE 20, 1782 - UNITED STATES

On July 4, 1776, the 1st committee was appointed to design a seal for the new country. Their design was tabled as was the design from the 2nd committee established in 1780. In 1782 Charles Thompson, Secretary of the Continental Congress, introduced this design for the new Seal of the United States. He told the members of Congress:

*"The colors of the pales are those used in the flag of the United States of America; White signifies purity and innocence, Red, hardiness and valour, and Blue, the color of the Chief signifies vigilance, perseverance and justice."*

On June 20, 1782 Congress approved the design, and the Great Seal of the United States was born. The image of the eagle within the seal became our National "Coat of Arms". One contributor to the design was Francis Hopkinton.

An official seal was needed for the upcoming Treaty of Paris which was signed the following year on September 3, 1783.

## SEPTEMBER 11, 1782 – CITY OF WHEELING WV

Elizabeth Zane, better known as "Betty Zane," is hailed as a heroine of the Revolutionary War for her defense of Fort Henry in the wilderness of western Virginia. On September 11, 1782, Fort Henry was besieged by the British and their Native American allies. Betty Zane was among those trapped inside. The attackers greatly outnumbered the defenders: 250 Native American warriors allied with 50 exceptionally able British soldiers who never had been defeated. Inside Fort Henry, there were only about 20 males of fighting age. Worse, they soon found themselves running out of gunpowder.

Betty Zane volunteered to leave the fort, return to her cabin 60 yards away and return to the fort with gunpowder.

Betty Zane's cunning and bravery saved Fort Henry from seizure by the Native Americans and British. Her act of heroism furthered the Revolutionary cause, not only by protecting Fort Henry, but also by proving that girls contributed to it as well. Her bravery is immortalized in a book written by her descendant, the famous writer Zane Grey, entitled *Betty Zane* (1903).

# APRIL 19, 1783 – TOWN OF NEW WINDSOR NY

During much of the Revolutionary War, New Windsor served as the major depot for the Continental Army and Army Medical Dept. In October 1782, the troops began to arrive and set up tents, while they began building their huts. This encampment or cantonment covered 1600 acres and quartered 6000-8000 men, women and children from New York, New Jersey, New Hampshire, Massachusetts and Maryland.

In order to reward the fidelity and faithfulness of three soldiers, Gen Washington ordered the establishment of an honor, the Badge of Merit be bestowed on them.

Eight years to the day when hostilities began in Lexington and Concord, Washington issued the cease fire orders here on April 19, 1783.

The Seal of the Town of New Windsor shall have inscribed therein, in circular form, the words "Town of New Windsor, Orange County, New York," and within the circle so formed shall be placed a replica of the Continental Soldier holding a bugle to his mouth with a flag attached. Under the sentinel, the Continental Soldier, shall be the inscription "1763."

218

# NOVEMBER 25, 1783 - NEW YORK CITY NY

Celebrated in NY for over 100 years as Evacuation Day, the British finally left New York City on this date in 1783. As they left, George Washington and his army entered New York to cheers and thousands of American flags.

An unidentified young Manhattan woman wrote in her dairy,

> *"We had been accustomed for a long time to military display in all the finish and finery of [British] garrison life. The troops just leaving us were as if equipped for a show and with their scarlet uniforms and burnished arms made a brilliant display. The troops that marched in, on the contrary, were ill-clad and weather-beaten and made a forlorn appearance. But then, they were our troops and as I looked at them and thought upon all they had done and suffered for us, my heart and my eyes were full."*

The seal of New York City is one of the oldest in NY dating from 1686. The only change to the seal occurred in 1784 after the Revolutionary War when the Imperial crown atop the hemisphere was replaced by an American eagle.

*The City of New York Seal is used with the permission from the City of New York.*

# ACKNOWLEDGEMENTS

I would like to thank the following people who were extremely helpful in obtaining high resolution images and background information on their municipality's contribution to the War and the significance of the illustrations in their seal or logo:

CONNECTICUT
      CITY OF DANBURY – Mayor Mark D. Boughton/Eliza Munoz, Communications Coordinator
      CITY OF GROTON – Debra Patrick, City Clerk
      CITY OF NEW HAVEN – Town website
      CITY OF NORWALK – Mayor Richard Moccia/ city website
      CITY OF WEST HAVEN – Mike Walsh, Public Information Officer
      TOWN OF BLOOMFIELD – Santerria Moore, Town of Bloomfield /Fredrick Hespeth, Historian
      TOWN OF COVENTRY- Laura Stone, Office of Town Manager
      TOWN OF GREENWICH – John Crary, Town Administartor
      TOWN OF GROTON – Janet L Downs, Deputy Town Clerk
      TOWN OF DURHAM – Alicia C. Fonash-Willett, Asst Town Clerk
      TOWN OF EAST HAVEN – Stacy Monico, Office of the Mayor
      TOWN OF LEBANON – Patti Handy, Office of the First Selectmen/Alicia Wayland, Town Historian
      TOWN OF RIDGEFIELD – Barbara, Town Clerk
      TOWN OF SALISBURY – Patricia Williams, Town Clerk
      TOWN OF SOUTHBURY – Town website 2011
      TOWN OF TRUMBULL – Suzanne Burr Monaco, Town Clerk
      TOWN OF WASHINGTON – Sheila Anson, Town Clerk
      TOWN OF WESTPORT – Gail Kelly, Asst Town Attorney/
      TOWN OF WETHERSFIELD – Jeff Bridges, Town Manager/ Amy, Historical Society

DELAWARE
      CITY OF WILMINGTON – Constance Cooper, Chief Curator Delaware Historical Society

GEORGIA
      CITY OF SAVANNAH – Luciana M. Spracher, Archivist City of Savannah Research Library
      GWINNETT COUNTY – Debra White, Gwinnett County
      HART COUNTY – Lawana Kahn, Hart County

INDIANA
      CITY OF VINCENNES – Dan Ravellatte, City of Vincennes
      TOWN OF CLARKSVILLE – website / Clarksville Historical Society

KENTUCKY
      CITY OF LOUISVILLE – Chris Poynter, Communications, Office of the Mayor

MAINE
      CITY OF PORTLAND – Margo McCain, Portland Public Library
      TOWN OF KITTERY – Jon Carter, Town Manager /
      TOWN OF WINSLOW – Town website
      TOWN OF YORK – Town website

# ACKNOWLEDGEMENTS

MARYLAND
    CHARLESTOWN – Linda Jackson, Town Clerk /Arch McKown, Historical Society Cecil County
    CHESTERTOWN – Wm Ingersoll, Town Supervisor
    HARFORD COUNTY – Harford County website

MASSACHUSETTS
    CHARLESTOWN – Carl Zellner, Allen Crawford
    CITY OF BOSTON- public domain
    CITY OF CAMBRIDGE – public domain
    CITY OF GARDNER – Alan Agnelli, City Clerk
    CITY OF NEW LONDON – City website
    CITY OF REVERE – Ashley Melnik, City Clerk
    CITY OF SOMERVILLE – City website
    TOWN OF ACTON – City website
    TOWN OF ARLINGTON – Clarissa Rowe, Chair, Board of Selectmen /
    TOWN OF BEDFORD – Town website
    TOWN OF BOXBOROUGH – Elizabeth Markiewicz, Town Clerk
    TOWN OF BURLINGTON – Amy Warfield, Town Clerk
    TOWN OF CHELMSFORD – Paul Cohen, Town Manager
    TOWN OF CONCORD – Anita Tekle, Town Clerk/ Board of Selectmen
    TOWN OF DANVERS – Judy Smith, Town of Danvers
    TOWN OF GARDNER – Alan Agnelli, City Clerk
    TOWN OF IPSWICH – Robert Markel, Town Manager
    TOWN OF KINGSTON – Town website
    TOWN OF LEXINGTON – Donna Hooper, Town Clerk/ Hank Manz, Board of Selectmen
    TOWN OF LINCOLN – Timothy Higgens, Town Administrator
    TOWN OF MARBLEHEAD – public domain (previous design before 1908)
    TOWN OF NORWOOD – Town website
    TOWN OF PLYMPTON – John Henry, Chairman, Board of Selectmen / Christine Maiorano,
                Plympton Historical Society
    TOWN OF PROVINCETOWN – Doug Johnstone, Town Clerk/ Town Selectmen
    TOWN OF SHARON – website public domain
    TOWN OF TEWKSBURY – Mary-Ann O Nichols, Town Clerk

NEW HAMPSHIRE
    CITY OF PORTSMOUTH – City website
    TOWN OF AUBURN – Joanne Linxweiler, Town Clerk / William Herman, Town Administrator
    TOWN OF DERRY – Town website
    TOWN OF DUNBARTON – Town website
    TOWN OF NEW BOSTON –Town website
    TOWN OF NEW CASTLE –Town website
    CITY OF NASHUA – City website
    TOWN OF NOTTINGHAM – Sandra Weston, Board of Selectman

# ACKNOWLEDGEMENTS

NEW JERSEY
    CITY OF ENGLEWOOD – City website
    CITY OF HACKENSACK – Albert H. Dib, Municipal Historian/legal Analyst
    CITY OF TRENTON – public domain
    BOROUGH OF BOUND BROOK – Cindy Tierney,
    BOROUGH OF CLOSTER – Mayor Heymann
    BOROUGH OF ENGLISHTOWN – Peter Gorbatuk, Town Clerk
    BOROUGH OF FORT LEE – Tom Meyers, Ft Lee Film Comm.
    BOROUGH OF LITTLE FERRY – Barbara Maldenado, Borough Clerk/Mayor and Council
    BOROUGH OF PAULSBORO – Marc Kamp, Director Economic Development
    BOROUGH OF RIVER EDGE – Judy O'Connell, Deputy Borough Clerk
    BOROUGH OF ROSELLE – Borough website
    BOROUGH OF RINGWOOD – Laurel Kidd, Borough of Ringwood
    BOROUGH OF WILDWOOD CREST – Janelle M. Holzmer, Deputy Municipal Clerk
    BOROUGH OF WOODLAND PARK – Thomas Minella, Sec to the Mayor
    MANALAPAN TOWNSHIP – Lydia Wykoff, Historian
    MERCER COUNTY – County website
    TOWN OF NEW HOPE – Town website
    TOWNSHIP OF EWING – Kim Marcellero, Deputy Municipal Clerk
    TOWN OF GREEN BROOK – Town website
    TOWNSHIP OF BEDMINSTER – Town website
    TOWNSHIP OF FRANKLIN –Town  website
    TOWNSHIP OF FREEHOLD – Cheryl Cook, Historian
    TOWNSHIP OF HOPEWELL – Town website
    TOWNSHIP OF PARSIPPANY TROY HILLS – Office of the Mayor
    TOWNSHIP OF PRINCETON – Linda McDermott, Town Clerk
    TOWNSHIP OF RIVERDALE – Township website
    TOWNSHIP OF SPRINGFIELD – Anthony Cancro, Township Administrator

NEW YORK STATE
    CITY OF BEACON – Brian Kelly, City of Beacon/Bob Murphy, Beacon Historical Soc
    CITY OF JOHNSTOWN – Cathy VanAlstyne, City Clerk
    CITY OF NEWBURGH – Elizabeth Evans, Asst City Admin /Richard Herbek, Acting City Mgr /
        Mary McTammany, City Historian
    CITY OF RENSSELAER – Mayor Dan Dwyer / Author Ernie Mann
    CITY OF ROME – Maureen Entelisano, Secretary to the Mayor
    CITY OF WHITE PLAINS – City website
    COUNTY OF CHEMUNG – County website
    HERKIMER COUNTY – Joanne Boyer, Herkimer County IT
    MONTGOMERY COUNTY – County website
    NEW YORK CITY – Mark Daly, Communications
    SARATOGA COUNTY – Jennifer Ciulla, Publication Spec./Barbara J. Plummer, Clerk of the Board
    TOWN OF ASHLAND – Town website
    TOWN OF FISHKILL – Willa Skinner, Historian
    TOWN OF FORT EDWARD – Linda A. Miles, Town Clerk
    TOWN OF GREENBURGH – Town website
    TOWN OF HORSEHEADS – Town website
    TOWN OF HOOSICK – Susan Stradinger, Town Clerk

# ACKNOWLEDGEMENTS

NEW YORK STATE (continued)

    TOWN OF KENT – Sallie Sypher, Putnam County

    TOWN OF KIRKLAND – Richard Williams, Historian

    TOWN OF LEICESTER – Gary Moore, Town Supervisor/ Tom Roffe, Town Historian

    TOWN OF NEW WINDSOR – Glen Marshall, Historian, Town of New Windsor

    TOWN OF NORTH CASTLE – town website

    TOWN OF PATTERSON – Michael Griffin, Town Supervisor

    TOWN OF PAWLING – Town website

    TOWN OF PELHAM – Jessica Hynes, Deputy Town Clerk, Blake Bell, Town Clerk

    TOWN OF PHILIPSTOWN – Tina Merando, Town Clerk

    TOWN OF SARATOGA – Thomas A. Wood III, Town Supervisor

    TOWN OF PUTNAM VALLEY – Sallie Sypher, Deputy Putnam County Historian

    TOWN OF STILLWATER – Linda Palmeri, Town Historian

    TOWN OF STONY POINT – Jane Skinner, Town Clerk

    TOWN OF WARWICK – Town website

    TOWN OF WESTMORELAND    Beverly Merriman, Town Clerk

    TOWN OF YORKTOWN – Alice Roker, Town Clerk

    VILLAGE OF CLINTON – Richard Williams, Historian

    VILLAGE OF HASTINGS-ON-HUDSON

    VILLAGE OF HORSEHEADS – Sharron Cunningham

    VILLAGE OF FISHKILL - Willa Skinner, Historian

    VILLAGE OF FORT PLAINS – Town Clerk

    VILLAGE OF PORT JEFFERSON – portjeffguide.com

    VILLAGE OF TARRYTOWN – Carol Booth, Town Clerk / Richard Miller, Historian

    VILLAGE OF WHITEHALL – Carol Greeno, Whitehall Historical Society

NORTH CAROLINA

    CITY OF CHARLOTTE – Gwendoln Jenkins, Office Manager, City Manager's Office

    CITY OF KINGS MOUNTAIN – Ellis Noell, Director of Special Events

    CITY OF MORGANTON - City website

    CITY OF GREENSBORO – City website

    HALIFAX COUNTY – County website

    MECKLENBURG COUNTY – Bill Carroll, Mecklenburg County

    TOWN OF ELIZABETHTON - Jennifer Nye, Town of Elizabethtown

    TOWN OF SUMMERFIELD – Town website

    TOWN OF WILKESBORO – Town website

OHIO

    CLARK COUNTY – Ben Sowards

PENNSYLVANIA

    BOROUGH OF BRIDGEPORT – Anthony DiSanto, Jr., Borough Manager

    BOROUGH OF HATBOROUGH - website

    BOROUGH OF PROSPECT PARK – Deb

    CHADDS FORD TOWNSHIP - website

    CITY OF PHILADELPHIA – Public Domain

    PAOLI – Bruce Knapp, President Paoli Battlefield Preservation Fund

    SKIPPACK TOWNSHIP – Del Locke, Township Manager

# ACKNOWLEDGEMENTS

WHITEMARSH TOWNSHIP - Mike Zeock, Community Service Coordinator, Whitemarsh Twnshp
YORK COUNTY – Steve Chronister, President Board of Commissioners

RHODE ISLAND
CITY OF NEWPORT – Edward Lavallee, City Manager, City of Newport
PAWTUXET VILLAGE - Village website
TOWN OF TIVERTON - Nancy Kelly, Town Clerk

SOUTH CAROLINA
CITY OF CAMDEN – Joanna Craig, Director /
CITY OF MANNING – Mayor Kevin Johnson / Col George Summers & Mrs. Summers
TOWN OF NINETY SIX – Town website
TOWN OF SULLIVAN'S ISLAND – Lisa Darrow, Asst Town Admin / Rick Hatcher, NPS

TENNESSEE
TOWN OF ELIZABETHTON – Fred Edens, J., City Manager

VERMONT
TOWN OF BENNINGTON – Town website

VIRGINIA
CITY OF RICHMOND – Carolyn Waller, Office of Press Secretary to the Mayor
CUMBERLAND COUNTY – Jennifer Roberts
CULPEPER COUNTY – Debbie Hoffman
FLUVANNA COUNTY- County Board of Supervisors (1987)
MATHEWS COUNTY – Deanna Harris, Administration
WASHINGTON COUNTY – Washington County
WESTMORELAND COUNTY – County Board of Supervisors
YORK COUNTY – York County
TOWN OF ABINGDON -Town of Abingdon
TOWN OF CULPEPER – Town of Culpeper
TOWN OF DUMFRIES – Lee C. Lansing Jr., Town Historian
TOWN OF WOODSTOCK – Town of Woodstock

WEST VIRGINIA
CITY OF POINT PLEASANT – Denny Bellamy, Director Mason County Tourism
CITY OF WHEELING – Judy Beabout, Sec to the City Mgr/ Margaret Brennan, Historian

ONEIDA INDIAN NATION – Deb Marino, Administrative Assistant

UNITED STATES
US ARMY – J Scott Chaffin, Trademark and Copyright Atty., US Army Legal Services
US NATIONAL GUARD – public domain
US NAVY – Admiralty seal - public domain
US MARINES – Jessica E O'Haver – USMC Trademark Licensing Program
US POSTAL SERVICE – public domain
US SEAL – public domain

# APPENDIX

Virginia Resolves 1766 - Chestertown Resolves 1774 - Hanover Resolves 1774 - Bush River Resolves 1775 – Mecklenburg Declaration 1775 – Liberty Point Resolves 1775 – Halifax Resolves 1776 – Essence of Declaration of Independence 1776

## VIRGINIA RESOLVES 1766

The following articles prepared and offered by RICHARD HENRY LEE were passed by the patriots of that day at LEEDST0WN, Virginia, in the 27th day of February, 1766.

*"ROUSED BY DANGER, and alarmed at attempts, foreign and domestic, to reduce the people of this country to a state of abject and detestable slavery, by destroying that FREE and happy constitution of government, under which they have hiterto lived, --- WE, who subscribe this paper, have associated, and do bind ourselves to each other, to GOD; and to our country, by the firmest ties that RELIGION and virtue can frame, most sacredly and punctually to stand by, and with our lives and fortunes, to SUPPORT, MAINTAIN, and DEFEND each other in the observance and execution of these FOLLOWING ARTICLES: -*

*FIRST. We declare all due allegiance and obedience to our lawful Sovereign; George the Third, King of Great Britian. And we determine to the utmost of our power to preserve the laws, the peace and good order of this Colony, as far as is consistent with the preservation of our Constitutional rights and liberty.*

*SECONDLY. As we know it to be the Birthright priviledge of every British subject, (and of the people of Virginia as being such) founded on Reason, Law, and Compact; that he cannot be legally tried, but by his peers; and that he cannot be taxed, but by a consent of a Parliament, in which he is represented by persons chosen by the people and who themselves pay a, part of the tax they impose on others. If therefore, any person or persons shall attempt, by any action or proceeding, to deprive this Colony of those fundamental rights, we will immediately regard him or them, as the most dangerous enemy of the community; and we will go to any extremity, not only to prevent the success of such attempts, but to stigmatize and punish the offender.*

*THIRDLY. As the Stamp Act does absolutely direct the property of the people to be taken from them without their consent expressed by their representatives and as in many case it deprives the British American Subject of his right to trial by jury; we do determine, at every hazard, and, paying no regard to danger or to death, we will exert every faculty, to prevent the execution of the said Stamp Act in any instance whatsoever within this Colony. And every abandoned wretch, who shall be so lost to virtue and public good, as wickedly to contribute to the Introduction or fixture of the Stamp Act in this Colony, by using stampt paper, or by any other means, we will, with the utmost expedition, convince all such profligates that immediate danger and disgrace shall attend their prostitute purposes.*

*FOURTHLY. That the last article may most surely and effectually be executed, we engage to each other, that whenever it shall be known to any of this association, that any person is so conducting himself as to favor the introduction of the Stamp Act, that immediate notice shall be given to as many of the association as possible, and that every individual so informed of, shall, with expedition, repair to a place of meeting to be appointed as near the scene of action as may be.*

*FIFTHLY. Each associator shall do his true endeavor to obtain as many signers to this association, as he possibly can.*

*SIXTHLY.  If any attempt shall be made on the liberty or property of any associator for any action or thing to be done in consequence of this agreement, we do most solemnly bind ourselves by the sacred engagements above entered into, at the risk of our lives and fortunes to restore such associate to his liberty, and to protect him in the enjoyment of his property."*

*In testimony of the good faith with which we resolve to execute this association we have this 27th day of February 1766, in Virginia, put our hands and seals hereto.*

# CHESTERTOWN RESOLVES – MAY 1774 BY THE LOCAL SONS OF LIBERTY

*1st- RESOLVED, that we acknowledge his majesty George III, King of Great Britain, France and Ireland, to be our rightful and lawful sovereign to whom we owe and promise all dutiful allegiance and submission.*

*2nd – RESOLVED, that no duty or taxes can constitutionally be opposed on us, but by our own consent given personally, or by our own representatives.*

*3rd – RESOLVED, that the act of the British parliament of the 7th of George III, chapter 46, subjecting the colonies to a duty on tea, for the purpose of raising revenue in America, is unconstitutional, oppressive and calculated to enslave the Americas.*

*4th – RESOLVED, therefore, that whoever shall import, or in any way aid or assist in importing, or introducing from any part of Great Britain, or any other place whatsoever, into this town or country, any tea subject to the payment of a duty imposed by the aforesaid act of Parliament: or whoever shall willingly and knowingly sell, buy or consume, in any way assist with the sale, purchase or consumption of any tea imported as aforesaid subject to a duty, he or they, shall be stigmatized as enemies to the liberties of America.*

*5th – RESOLVED, that we will not only steadily adhere to the foregoing resolves, but will endeavor to excite our worthy neighbors to a like patriotic conduct, and to whoever, amongst, shall refuse his concurrence, or after complying, shall desert the cause, and knowingly deviate from the true spirit and meaning of these our resolutions, w will mark him out and inimical to the liberties of America, and unworthy member of the community, ad a person not deserving our notice our regard.*

*6th – RESOLVED, that the foregoing resolves be printed, that our brothers in the and other colonies may now our sentiments as therein contained.*

Signed by order of the Committee, W Wright, Clerk